PASPOORT.
KONINGRIJK DER NEDERLANDEN.

Ingevolge magtiging van het DEPARTEMENT VAN OORLOG, d.d. *11 December 1861*, n°. *83*, verleent de Kommanderende Officier van *het 8ᵉ Regiment Infanterie*, bij deze, PASPOORT aan den *milicien*

van der Schaaf Johannes

zoon van *Reinder Meints* en van *Doedtje Aukes Figchelaar* ; geboren te *Lollum (Wonseradeel)*, provincie *Friesland*, den *19 October 1842* ; laatst gewoond te *Arum (id)* ; lang *1 el 5 palm 7 duim 5 streep*; aangezigt *ovaal* voorhoofd *laag* oogen *blaauw* ; neus *breed*, mond *klein*, kin *spits*, haar *lichtbruin* wenkbraauwen *idem* merkbare teekenen *geene* ; stamboek n°. *52521* ; en zulks uithoofde van *geeindigde militie diensttijd*

Staat van dienst.

Bij het 8 Regiment Infanterie den 29 April 1861 ingedeeld als milicien voor den tijd van vijf jaren zijnde loteling van de ligting van 1861 uit de provincie Friesland gemeente Wonseradeel onder n°. 65 reserve 1 Januarij 1862 in de categorie van groot verlof overgebragt 22 Mei 1862 bij het Korps den 5 September 1862 met groot verlof 3 Augustus 1864 bij het Korps terug 13 September " met groot verlof

Gedane veldtogten, bekomen wonden, bijzondere daden, eereteekenen.

Met bovengemelden persoon is afgerekend en ~~aan hem tot saldo van Rekening~~ uitbetaald de som van *——*, welke hij verklaart te hebben ontvangen.

Alle burgerlijke en militaire autoriteiten worden verzocht genoemden gepasporteerde vrij en ongehinderd te laten passeren, en hem, zoo noodig, hulp en bijstand te verleenen.

Handteekening
van den gepasporteerde,

J R v d Schaaf

Te *Leeuwarden* den *28 April* 1800 *zes* en zestig.

De Kolonel
Winsack

Art. 13 der wet van 19 Augustus 1861 (Staatsblad n°. 78).

Stamboek-nommer *52521*

CERTIFICAAT VAN GOED GEDRAG.

(1) *8ᵉ Regiment Infanterie*

De Kommanderende Officier van gemeld korps verklaart, bij deze, dat de gepasporteerde (2) *milicien Johannes van der Schaaf* zich, gedurende zijn diensttijd, goed heeft gedragen.

Te *Leeuwarden* den *28 April* 1866.

De Kolonel
Winsack

(1) Benaming van het korps.
(2) Hoedanigheid, voornaam en naam.

This passport was issued to John R. Van Der Schaaf who migrated to Sioux County in 1872

1

The Prairie Had Never Been Dis

urbed And It Held Great Promise

The History of Orange City 1870 – 1970

Iowa had been a state for only one year when the first of the Orange City pioneers emigrated from the Netherlands to America in 1847. Under the leadership of Rev. H. P. Scholte, the first Dutch settlers in Iowa established a colony at Pella; Although fresh from Holland, with its tiny fields, dykes, canals, and flat land, the pioneers soon adapted to Iowa and prospered in the wide open plains.

Conditions in Holland were such that the working man could not afford the ordinary staples of life like meat and wheat bread. He depended mostly on the humble potato as his staff of life. A disease destroyed the potato crop in 1845 and again in 1846 and 1847. To meet the problems of poverty and food shortage, plans were made to send farmers as emigrants to Surenam in South America, the East Indies, or America. After careful study, America was selected. Some Dutch people had already settled at various places there, and had written glowing reports of this land where people enjoyed social equality and full freedom of religion — two basic rights sorely lacking in Holland.

In the mid 1800's there were serious religious conflicts in Holland. The Reformed doctrine was ridiculed as old-fashioned and out of date, and its followers were persecuted, despised and mistreated. Reformed Church leaders were sometimes imprisoned. After Rev. Scholte spent three weeks in jail, his congregation decided to emigrate to America. There seemed to be no future for them in Holland. From the many applicants, those chosen were nearly all from well-to-do agricultural classes — farmers who owned and tilled their own land, and who were sober, industrious, and moral citizens.

The people who came to Pella and Sioux County at that time and in the succeeding years left established homes and loved ones behind. Many never saw their family or old friends again. In crowded, primitive ships they braved the perils of the Atlantic Ocean voyage. Traveling emigrant class rather than first class on the voyage of up to two months, many families lost loved ones enroute, loved ones buried at sea. The family of John Hospers, father of Orange City pioneer Henry Hospers, lost two children while crossing the ocean, and a third child died after they arrived in New York.

The E. J. G. Bloemendaal and Gerrit Hofmeyer families suffered a ship-wreck in the wind-tossed waters of a terrible storm. They were able to save only a small bundle of clothes, but no family members lost their lives. After their rescue by two other ships, they watched in horror as some of their fellow passengers sank to a watery grave.

When the colonists landed, they were strangers in a strange land and knew neither its language nor its customs. Those determined Hollanders, however, were held in high regard and were treated with favor by fellow Christian believers and by State Officials and State Assemblies. It was said that they resembled the God-fearing pilgrims, and their coming to America was considered a blessing.

Sick and weakened by the voyage, the settlers landed at bustling ports. Many landed at Baltimore, where the streets were muddy, and chickens, hogs, and cattle roamed at will. It was a marked contrast to the cobbled streets and the orderly, neat towns to which they had been accustomed.

Never before from the flat lowlands of Holland, the travelers' first experiences with the steep inclines and tunnel passages of mountain travel left them awed and amazed. With hardy determination they crossed the Cumberland Gap and traveled by boat and barge down the Ohio River and then up the Mississippi to St. Louis. There they waited until a site could be chosen for the colony. A Presbyterian congregation offered the newcomers the use of their church for worship and Sunday School services. Conditions were worsened by unsanitary conditions, a dreadful heat wave, and an inability to communicate with those about them.

Finally, it was on to Keokuk where the weary travelers bought covered wagons, horses, and oxen and other equipment to enable them to proceed to Pella. An early Dutch writing reports that Matthys De Booy bought a wagon and team of horses for $250.00 to make the trip.

The colonists finally arrived in Pella, their city of refuge. In spite of untold hardships there, the colony grew and prospered. One of the colonists, Mr. Sjoerd Aukes Sipma, wrote glowing letters to his relatives in Holland. Perhaps there was exaggerated optimism in the letters, but they were published in a local Netherlands paper, where they created such interest that many more decided to emigrate to America. A few of those letters can be found today in the Archives at the Hague.

As the Pella area developed, railroads were built and speculators got set for great profiteering. Land was selling for thirty to sixty dollars per acre, prices which made the conservative Dutch hesitate.

Jelle Pelmulder, who had been a schoolmaster at Beernward in Friesland, had emigrated to Iowa in 1856 and had acquired a farm eight miles north of Pella. In 1867 he began to discuss the necessity of starting a new settlement. Interest was aroused and meetings followed, after he corresponded with land offices and secured encouraging information.

Mr. Henry Hospers

Mr. and Mrs. H. J. Vande Waa

Pelmulder got his old friend Sjoerd Sipma interested, and Hendrick Jan Van De Waa, a Civil War Veteran who had been in Pella since 1847, also became very enthusiastic about a new settlement. He was tired of high prices and soaring rents. After corresponding with a land agent in Storm Lake, he was informed that Homesteads were still available in Northwest Iowa.

Mr. Van De Waa decided to sell his property in Pella and take advantage of the homestead benefits. He went to the newspaper office of Henry Hospers, then mayor of Pella, to have his auction bills printed. Hospers, who had been thinking for some time of starting a new colony, had his interest kindled anew. He also wrote to Storm Lake and received nothing but favorable replies. Meetings were called, and so much interest was shown that it was decided to send a committee to investigate the possibility of obtaining a large, inexpensive tract of land for a new colony in Northwestern Iowa.

The committee was comprised of Sjoerd Aukes Sipma, Jelle Pelmulder, Huibertus Muilenburg, and Hendrick Jan Van De Waa. Van De Waa offered his wagon and team. The wagon was converted into a prairie schooner by stretching a white canvass over bows of wood six feet high to give protection from sun and rain. Provisions were packed for a four-week trip, and by April 26, 1869, the explorers were ready to set off. A short time before, Van De Waa had traded his team of horses for a young span of mules. The mules had never worn a harness, and by kicking and struggling for two hours, they tried to prove that harnesses were not for them. With a joint effort, however, the men succeeded in harnessing the mules and hitching them to the wagon. All four men jumped into the wagon and left Pella at a near-runaway pace for the first few miles. In anticipation of possible further difficulties, the harnesses were never removed until the return trip. By that time the

The mules had never worn a harness, and by kicking and struggling for two hours they tried to prove that harnesses were not for them. In anticipation of possible difficulties, the harnesses were never removed until the return trip.

mules were well broken and gentle, a tribute to the spirit and courage of the early pioneers.

After the explorers passed through Newton and Webster City, they joined an emigrant train at Fort Dodge. All along the way they made inquiries to settling places and soil fertility. Swollen rivers, creeks, and sloughs without bridges were difficult and dangerous to cross, but the men continued across the roadless countryside on to Storm Lake. Only by following a compass and a few scattered railroad survey markers were they able to keep their bearings. Upon reaching Cherokee, the four men were told of land available to the west. The area was sufficient in size, and the type of soil was to their liking, so they decided they had found the land where they would settle. Immediately, the determined emigrants headed for

the land office at Sioux City. There, a throng of land seekers crowded them out, and they were unable to gain admittance until that evening, when an official heard of their intentions and was kind enough to admit them through the back door. The four explorers could report only intentions, since there were no binding agreements with any of the folks back in Pella. But the land office authorities encouraged them, and they hurried back to Pella to report their findings. There the response was so great that 86 applications for homesteads were filed, and further requests were made for outright purchase of land.

An association for colonization was formed with a membership of eighty-two persons, and a new committee consisting of Henry Hospers, Leendert Vander Meer, Dirk Vanden Bos, and Hendrick Jan

Van De Waa was appointed. Vande Waa again offered his wagon and mules. This time he was paid two dollars and fifty cents per day for furnishing the transportation. The new committee was given authority to act on its own, without referring back to the Association.

If the site at Cherokee proved too small, the committee members were given the power to select another site. They were instructed to distribute the Homesteaders in such a way that relatives would be able to live near one another. The date set for departure was June 14, 1869, and the association members were to have their money paid in by that date.

Mr. Hospers went ahead by rail to Sioux City to obtain all necessary information. The others then followed the trail taken by the previous committee. Vander Meer and Vanden Bos had recently returned from Oregon where they had gone with a wagon train led by Cornelius Jongewaard in 1864. On hearing of colonization plans, they returned to Pella on the newly-completed Union Pacific Railroad. With their six-month trip on the Oregon trail behind them, they were seasoned travelers for the new undertaking.

Big disappointment faced these men when they met at Sioux City. Land speculators had gained knowledge of the Hollanders earlier plans and had purchased the entire area near Cherokee, hoping to net a nice profit by reselling the land to the Hollanders. Instead of falling prey to speculation strategy, the committee decided to explore other areas further north. They were told at Sioux City about Sioux and Lyon Counties, where government and railroad land was still available. They obtained maps, compasses, and surveying equipment, engaged a surveyor, and packed provisions for a three-week trip. Traveling north, they entered Sioux County where Sherman and Nassau Townships meet, just six miles south and two miles west of the present Northwestern College corner.

When the four men saw the land before them, they agreed with one accord that they need go no farther. They were silent, reverent, and deeply stirred at the sight before them—beautiful, gently rolling hills of prairie with the Floyd River lazily meandering through its verdant grass. Nature and the virgin prairie had never been disturbed. Violets, roses, buttercups, and daisies added sparkle to the beautiful landscape they were scanning. Small priarie animals eyed them curiously, and the deep, black soil held out its promise of abundant productivity. Here they would build their homes. This indeed was for them the Promised Land.

Very shortly, the industrious men began measuring in a northerly direction, continuing until they came to the West Branch of the Floyd River just west of what is now the village of Middleburg. There they found a large body of water later named Bells Lake which is now dry tillable farm land.

Near Bells Lake the four committeemen raised pyramids of dirt on the hill tops as markers so they would not get lost. They marked two townships, and then they turned south and selected the excellent hill-top site for the town which is now Orange City.

The men returned to Sioux City where the Homesteads were assigned as previously agreed. Vander Meer, Vanden Bos, and Van De Waa returned to Pella while Henry Hospers remained in Western Iowa for a few days to attend to legal matters.

On his return to Pella, Hospers gave glowing accounts and stated that during his 22 years in America, he had never seen a more beautifully situated stretch of country. He also explained how Homesteads could be acquired under the laws of the United States and urged people to take advantage of the opportunity.

Early in September, 1869, seventy-five men, including three surveyors, loaded 18 wagons with provisions and made the three-hundred-mile trip to their future farms. They carried out the requirements of the Homestead Laws, plowed furrows around their claims, and then returned home to prepare for a permanent move the next spring. The "Mother" Colony of Pella then would have a "Daughter" Colony. The same names were found in both colonies because some of the original colonists, or their descendants were continuing on to Sioux County. They were ready to endure again the hardships of establishing a new settlement.

The Wagon Trains Leave Pella

H. J. Van De Waa led the first wagon train out of Pella. With him were G. Vander Steeg, Arie Vander Meide, H. J. Luymes, and the Beukelom Brothers with their mother and sister. A second train had Pelmulder as the leader and consisted of Friesian families. Sixty wagons made up the third wagon train, which was headed by Leendert Vander Meer and Dirk Vanden Bos. At each departure, a large crowd of well wishers gathered to see the pioneers off. Prayers were offered and Psalms and hymns were sung. The last hymn sung was entitled, "In the Sweet Bye and Bye."

The covered prairie schooners were drawn by horses or mules, or by two or three yoke oxen teams. Although slower the oxen were more dependable in drawing the wagons through miry sloughs. Bridges were few and entirely lacking toward the end of the trip. In the Van De Waa train the Beukelom wagon was the fifth in line. The first four wagons crossed a bridge safely in a zig-zag manner, but the Beukelom wagon, with mother and daughter, started straight across. Beukelom was not the best driver, and the team he was driving was partially blind. The flooring of the bridge was loose. In some way or other, from the loose flooring of the bridge the wagon toppled downward some twelve feet. Fortunately, there was only two feet of water, and the passengers were only slightly bruised. But their clothing was soaked, and a crate full of chickens drowned. After some roadside and riverside repair, the procession was able to continue its journey. Often times a wagon would bog down to the hubs, and then several yokes of oxen would be hitched up to draw the wagon to more solid ground. The travelers crossed many miles of green, rolling prairie before they reached their destination. Early each morning they broke camp. At noon they stopped for lunch, and each evening came the toilsome task of setting up camp for the night. Grace was said before each meal, and a prayer of Thanksgiving followed. On Sundays, the pioneers rested from the exhausting travel; sermons were read, prayers offered, and Psalms sung.

The Van De Waa and Pelmulder trains reached Sioux County after nineteen days of travel. Others took more days still to cover the distance now driven in about five smooth hours.

Following are the names of the pioneers who, with their families, left Pella for their new home in Sioux County in April and May 1870. (Listed in the Pella Book)
*Indicates leaders of wagon trains.

Beyer, Gerrit	Jong, de K. Kz	Rooijen, van Wouter
Berge van den Ads	Klein, Johannes	Ruisch, de D.
Beukelman, Mrs	Lakeman, Cornelius	Rysdam, G.
Boersma, H.	Lenderink, A.	Rysdam, W.
Boersma, L.	Logterman, J.	Schippers, A.
*Bos, van den Dirk	Luymes, H. J.	Sinnema, J.
Brinks, J.	Marel, van Arie	Steeg, van der Gerrit
Brower, Tjeerd	*Meer, van der Dirk	Steenwyk, van Abraham
Dielman, Pieter	Meer, van der J.	Talsma, Ryn
Fennema, J.	*Meer, van der Leendert	Verheul, Maarten
Gorter, J.	*Meide, van der Arie	Versteeg, Arie
Groen, Jan	Muilenburg, Jacob	*Waa, van der H. J.
Haan, de Wopke	Nieuwendorp, Christian	Werkhoven, Arie
Hartog, den Hyme	Noteboom, Arie	Wieringa, K.
Heemstra, T.	Pas, Huibert	Windhorst, J.
Horsen, van Pieter	*Pelmulder, Jelle	Wyk, van Johannes
Iperen, van I.	Pelt, Van Leendert	Wynia, Ulbe
Jong, de P. Kz.	Pelt, van der Dirk	Zalm, van der Wm.
Jong, de O.	Ploeg, van der Ipe	Zeeuw, de G.
Jongewaard, Cornelius	Pool, S.	Zante, van D. Hz.
Jansma, Ane	Raad, de Arie	Zyl, van der Bart

The Crucial First Years

On reaching Sioux County, the Van De Waa train camped the first night near what was called the Orange City slough, located about one half mile north of Orange City. With the aid of compasses and maps, the colonists set out to find their claims. The surveyor's traces made the previous year were found undisturbed. The very first day in the new settlement, two men were seen digging a cellar near a wagon load of building lumber. Nearby, a number of cattle and some yoke of oxen grazed on the priarie. The Pella travelers soon learned that the two men were Tjeerd Heemstra and his son who had come from the Michigan settlement. At the Sioux City Land Office Heemstra had filed on a still open claim about one-half mile south of what is now Northwestern College. They had come from Chicago in ox-drawn wagons and had met the Vander Meer train on the way.

For all the pioneers, the chief task was to break the priarie. Each Homesteader turned enough sod to produce a small crop. Then each year more sod was broken into tillable land. Every farmer walked long miles behind his plow which turned only a 14-inch furrow. Seed potatoes were thrust between the strips, and gopher and prairie dog mounds became seed beds for vegetables such as lettuce, radishes, beans, carrots, and cabbage.

At first, all the seed was sown by hand from a large bag hung from the sower's shoulder. The grain, mostly wheat, was cut by hand with a scythe. Then the windrows were gathered into bundles and tied with stems of joined straw. Later the grain was beat out with flails and put into sacks.

During the first summer months, many of the colonists used their wagons for sleeping quarters and lived in tents while preparing sod houses or dug-outs. Lumber had to be hauled 20 miles from Le Mars. Rivers and sloughs, which had to be crossed every trip, at times were impossible in spring and summer when streams were in flood stage. That part of the trip was easier in winter, when the ground and streams were frozen solid.

For their early homes, the first settlers would dig a hole about five feet deep preferably on the east or south side of a slope. Then they raised sod walls above the ground. The roofs, framed with poles cut from trees, were covered with long slough grass and then another layer of sod. A small window at each end was the only light, and the door was like a trap door, with steps leading up to it. Often a ledge was left along the inside of the dug-out wall to provide seating space. Willows and box elders were hauled from the Floyd River for use as framing and lumber. Depending on the re-sources of the homemaker, some of the sod homes became remarkably attractive and comfortable. Some even had two rooms. The furniture was simple—a dry goods box could serve as a wardrobe, cupboard, or table. But some of the pioneers lived in these humble homes for several years. Babies were even born in a few of the dug outs, often only with the help of a neighbor lady who became a sort of self-made nurse.

The grandchildren of E. J. G. Bloemendaal like to tell of an experience their grandparents had with their dug-out. Mr. Bloemendaal built one in 1871. In 1872 he brought a new bride from Michigan over to his sod hut. He had not exactly informed her of what she might expect. One night there was a severe thunder storm, and rain poured down in torrents. After the wind damaged the roof, the young couple put up an umbrella to try to stay dry. Even the flame in their oil lamp was extinguished. The following beautiful, sunshiny day, the young pioneers waded into their house to remove their wet belongings, and then they scopped out the water. That dug-out was replaced in the fall with a more conventional house. The following winter Bloemendaal's brother arrived from the Netherlands. Through some mistake of the Railroad Company their bedding was delayed seven weeks. In the meantime, since there was only one bed, the two couples had to sleep in turns.

Once their families were housed, the pioneers began building shelters for the animals and cribs for crops. The Rock and Sioux Rivers, 20 miles west, were the best source of building lumber. At those rivers, the settlers got seddlings of cotton-wood, maple, oak, and ash trees. The seedlings were planted on their homesteads so that one day they might enjoy their own wind breaks and shade trees. Wood also was used as fuel, supplementing the use of corn stalks, cobs, grass, and even cow dung. Coal was not only expensive, it had to be hauled in from Le Mars.

Some settlers were able to build frame houses complete with two rooms and a loft which could only be reached with a ladder. But even these frame homes would allow the snow to sift in, and sometimes the beds and blankets would be covered with snow in the morning after a blizzard. Fires could not be kept burning throughout the night, and water would freeze solid in the water pail. When water was spilled it would quickly freeze solid on the cold, frozen floors.

There were no stores, and all supplies had to be hauled in from Le Mars. An excursion to Le Mars was an all day trip, and supplies were usually brought for the neighbors too. Sacks of wheat were brought to Le Mars to be ground into flour or bartered for supplies. The Elkhorn Tavern, named after the big branding elkhorn fastened to the gable of the door, was a stopping place for many travelers. It was located two miles southwest of Orange City and was operated by Aaron Van Wechel. Sleeping places on the floor were provided, since there were often not enough beds.

Snowstorms struck without warning across the treeless prairies and raged with relentless fury. Sometimes they would come so suddenly that in a few minutes the pioneers could see less than ten feet ahead. On one such occasion, some men were cutting wood at the Rock River. Clouds formed, and snowflakes began to fall. The wood cutters hurried for home, but lost their way. One of the horses in the lead team had a colt at home, and when the horses stopped, they were in front of the barn which held the colt.

At another time five teams were on their way home from Le Mars. Shortly after noon, about five miles south of Orange City a snowstorm struck. Again the men depended on their horses, which eventually led them to a store building in Orange City. So severe were those blizzards that sometimes the settlers became lost going from the barn to the house, and they soon learned to put up guide ropes across the farm yard.

In 1871 Henry Hospers resigned as mayor of Pella. He sent contractor Gleysteen to Orange City to build a General Store on the lot where the Klay and Bastemeyer law office is now located. John and Simon Kuyper operated the store until Mr. Hospers himself came in May to run the business. Butter and eggs were bartered and exchanged for merchandise. Mr. Hospers was the chief promoter of the colony, and he was its leader in most business and official affairs. He was a land agent, notary public, and counsellor at law. Under his guidance, Orange City soon took on the aspects of a frontier village. The Tinch Hotel, a Blacksmith Shop, and a Livery Stable were built on what is now the Court House Square. A barbershop and shoe and harness shop were added and more houses were built.

In those days, the houses were unduly scattered— sometimes one on a block or even ten or twenty acres. Outbuildings were also necessary to provide for a horse, some pigs, a few cows, and some chickens. Every home owner had a large garden. Potatoes filled the cellar bins, and carrots, beets, and turnips were stored in sand. Sauerkraut kept best in crocks, and peas and beans were usually dried. The homemaker took great pride in providing for her family in this way, and seed was always saved for the next year's garden.

The Saint Paul and Sioux City Railroad, when it came through east Orange (now Alton), was an added boon to the colony's growth. It soon eliminated the necessity of making trips to Le Mars for most necessities.

Also in 1872, the Court House was forcibly moved to Orange City from Calliope (now Hawarden), and Orange City colonists active in politics won a number of county elections. Some of the office holders were Antonie J. Betten Jr., Auditor, Jelle Pelmulder, Clerk of District Court, J. W. Greatrax, Treasurer, and Henry Hospers and Tjeerd Heemstra, Board of Supervisors. The early official record books are filled with the beautiful, sometimes shaded, penmanship of some of these early public servants.

When Mrs. Henry Hospers went to visit at Pella that summer, she persuaded her husband's younger brother Cornelius to return with her. He arrived in Orange City in early November and noted that there were no sidewalks and only about a dozen houses in the town. Cornelius had had some college, and his brother Henry appointed him as school teacher beginning with the winter term. He was paid twenty-seven dollars per month, and he had sixty-nine pupils. A record of the students and their ages in the spring of 1873 has been preserved:

Antonie Betten	7	Samuel Muilenburg	10
Dirk Betten	14	Teunes Muilenburg	7
Simon Bolks	14	John Mak	8
William De Gooier	12	Cornelius Mouw	8
Isaac De Haan	14	Johanna Mouw	11
Mary De Haan	11	Gerrit Noteboom	16
John De Haan	9	Nellie Noteboom	12
Johanna De Kraay	11	John Noteboom	15
Katie Dingeman	12	Peter Noteboom	15
Effie Dingeman	10	Lena Nieuwendorp	14
Urdy Gorter	10	John Pas	13
Gerrit Hospers	8	Cornelius Vanden Bos	13
Maggie Hospers	5	John Vanden Bos	8
Peter Hospers	14	Ringert Rozeboom	9
Antonie Jongewaard	5	Henry Spaan	10
Catherine Jongewaard	5	Teutje Spaan	12
Denis Jongewaard	13	Lambert van Olst	10
Gysbert Jongewaard	10	Berdie Vande Steeg	13
John Jongewaard	17	Gysje G. D. Vande Steeg	13
Katie Jongewaard	12	Alida Vander Meer	9
Ring A. Jongewaard	15	Cornelia Vander Meer	14
William Jongewaard	10	Isaac Vander Meer	14
Roelof Menning	15	Jane Vander Meer	13
Alexander Muilenburg	14	Martin Vander Meer	11
Johanna Muilenburg	9	Lizzie Veldhuisen	11
Johanna Muilenburg	13	Henrietta Vande Steeg	10
John W. Muilenburg	15	Henry Vanden Berg	14
Isaac Muilenburg	15	John Vanden Berg	11
James Muilenburg	11	Hubert Walraven	12
Lizzie Muilenburg	12	Mary Walraven	9
Marie Muilenburg	9		

Other schools were built at random throughout the settlement, not on the center of four section blocks as they later were situated. In July of 1873 Abraham Lenderink was reported to be building six school houses.

The settlers continually improved their homes and living conditions. Frame dwellings soon replaced sod houses, and the pioneers bought needed clothings and other items which had previously been beyond their means. Railroad sections were listed on the market, and the settlers proceeded to buy the land before speculators grabbed it. Many of the struggling farmers were obliged to go into debt to buy the additional land, but they were considered trustworthy folks and their promissory notes were readily accepted. Always planning for the future, the farmers also purchased additional furnishings and equipment for their farms.

A Visit from Jesse James and His Men

Jesse James and his outlaw companions were in Orange City in the early 1870's. One night there was a knock at the door of the little home of Mr. and Mr. Arie Noteboom, a mile west of town. Three men with guns were standing at the door. When they requested care for their horses and lodging for the night, the young couple let them sleep in an upstairs room where supplies were stored. It was the best they had to offer. The Notebooms themselves did not get much sleep that night. The following morning the gang rode away without incident, while the Notebooms watched them from a window as far as they could see them go. Since Jesse James and his men were known to exchange their horses for better horses or for fresh ones when their mounts were tired, they caused the Notebooms anxious moments. All of the area settlers joined the unwilling hosts in thankful relief when the outlaws left the region.

Grasshoppers

One Sunday morning when the colonists were gathered at church services, they heard an unfamiliar whirring, pattering sound. Investigation disclosed that grasshoppers or Rocky Mountain Locusts were flying in from Minnesota toward the Southwest. The main wave appeared like a huge cloud and approached with a thunder-like roar. The sky darkened, and chickens went to roost. Grasshoppers were everywhere. By Monday morning, the ripening oats and wheat crops had been totally destroyed, and vegetables, corn, shrubbery, and even weeds fared no better. As many as 387 hoppers were reported clinging to a single cornstalk. Some colonists lost all, while some reaped a fourth of a crop, and most became destitute and short of food with winter just ahead.

The Iowa General Assembly appointed a committee to investigate the devastation in Sioux, Lyon, Osceola, and O'Brien counties. The committee found a deserving group of settlers—sincere, industrious, intelligent, and thrifty—who were not at all willing to resort to charity. In the end the Legislature appropriated $50,000 to be distributed by the county supervisors for the purchase of seed, grain, and vegetables.

The pioneer farmers planted again in the spring. In June all looked promising. The oats and wheat were about ready for harvest when, on Sunday, July 19, the locusts came again stripping forty to sixty miles in area. This second scourage put the settlers in still more destitute circumstances. Some sold out and moved away. One family, records indicate, sold an entire eighty acres for $225.00, including a span of mules, a wagon, and a cow. Others sold out in order to purchase a ticket for their return to Holland. Some just left. Mr. Hospers and Rev. Bolks did much to help these discouraged settlers. Those who remained have never regretted it and have been amply repaid for their courage. But more trials were in store. In 1875 there was a good crop except for some damage by storm. Then rust came into the wheat and oats, and the grain fell to the ground.

In 1876 the grasshoppers returned, and again in 1877, but the damage inflicted was not nearly as bad as the first year.

In 1878 there was a good crop, but rain storms flattened the grain so that it was difficult to harvest. It rained during the entire month of August and not until September 7 were the farmers able to gather in the wheat, much of which had sprouted and had little value. In 1879 drought and dust storms replaced the usual spring rains. In July more grasshoppers came, and then a thunderstorm and tornado came to climax the destruction.

DE VOLKSVRIEND.

XXIste Jaargang   ORANGE CITY, SIOUX COUNTY, IOWA, DONDERDAG. 19 SEPTEMBER, 1895.   Nommer 40

1874. 1895. DE VOLKSVRIEND. EENENTWINTIG JAREN. 't getal, dat in Bijbel- volmaaktheiï een go	schiedenis van den dag in de eerste tijden beschreef, en ten anderen om bij 't koniende geslacht de worsteling der "pioneers", en Gods goede hand over allen, in gedach- tenis te houden. Van alle "new ers" werd r ʳ gemaakt, ɔtie, ɔctie,	den roem der Hollanders te be- zingen ten koste van den goeden naam hnars petekinds, het toen- malige Calliope in zuidwest Sioux county. Niettemin—die sledorijdende hel- den zijn een epos waardig. 't Ging over de ongebaande sneeuw Van de een tot de andere farm; 't Vroor even tw ig onder nul, Maar 't eer dan warm, slechtr	nieuwe redakteur had vele beken- den in 't Oude Vaderland en aan velen zond hij zijn blad om hen in kennis te stellen met de goede land- streek hier, en met de goede kan- een zelfs voor niets bezittenden. Bovendien werden verschillende zijner beschou gen, zoowel over de kolonie al Amerikaansche kerkelijk ndige aange- le ʳl r door Ne-	harten volgende, zijn blad meer dienstbaar gemaakt hebben aan E- vangelisatie werk; maar om het te vergrooten en daardoor, behalve ruimte voor 't gewone nieuws, ook voldoende ruimte voor godsdien- stige stukken te verk was, wegens de voor hem wel kwam het	te Pella, een welgeredigeerd blad, welks bestaan tot veler smart in- dertijd al te plotseling werd afge- broken. Zooals te verwachten was zou de uitgave van Dᴇ Volks- vriend hem dur ʳ ɔuwd	

The Years of Growth

Mr. Henry Hospers began publishing "De Volks-vriend," a weekly newspaper, in 1874. Translated, the name means "Friend of the People." The Dutch language was used to help attract and encourage emigrants to come to Sioux County. From the records in the paper, by 1875 the Orange City settlement claimed 468 families—some 2,500 people. 30,000 acres were being tilled, and some 200,000 bushels of wheat were raised that year. A wind-driven gust, or genuine Dutch Windmill, was under construction for grinding the wheat into flour. "De Volksvriend" for many years enjoyed a wide circulation among Dutch settlements in many states.

In the autumn of 1875, a second booster trip was welcomed from Pella. For a group of 225 people, a round trip railroad ticket came to $5.50 each. On Hearing of the impending visit, the editor of the paper urged everyone to get singing groups together, put organs into shape, string the violins, get out the flags, and prepare decorations of flow-ers. Eighty vehicles were waiting at the depot in East Orange (Alton) when the visitors arrived, and a brass band furnished the evening's enter-ment. The next afternoon all gathered for a wor-ship service in the church. The two days of feasting and visiting were enjoyed by relatives and friends alike and served as encouragement and praise for the colony.

As the years passed, the local government began to assert itself. A new Courthouse was built in the public square in 1874, and in 1876 a jail was erect-ed. On land purchased to serve as a county poor farm, there is now the County Home northwest of town.

Stores meant a great deal to the early day settlers—they supplied everything from coffee to kerosene. Coffee beans at first, were ground at home, but later the stores kept grinders on the counter to provide fresh ground coffee. Crackers and pickles were kept and displayed in open barrels, and syrup was pumped from a barrel. Even in 50-pound sacks, flour was purchased several sacks at a time, since all bread was baked at home. Families, large and small, used the warm, fresh-baked bread as a staple part of their diet. In the stores there were no self-service arrangements. Clerks waited on their customers in those days. Most groceries came in bulk and were weighed out to the customer, and yards of dress goods were cut from huge bolts. In the fall heavy clothing, coats, and long underwear made up most shopping lists, in anticipation of the coming winter.

New business places were added to Orange City as the years passed. John Vande Steeg and Anthony Betten began business in 1879. Their store was destroyed by fire in 1900, and Mr. Betten, who carried no insurance, was unable to continue. Vande Steeg, however, rebuilt on the same location, and his department store remained in business until 1960—a total of eighty-one years. Dykema's store now occupies the building.

In 1882 Henry Hospers built a new bank building across the street east from the windmill park. It later became a Post Office, and is now occupied by DeHaan Electric. Gezelschap's Drug Store was located just to the north.

Orange City finally got a railroad line in 1882. That year the Chicago and Northwestern Railroad was built along the south edge of present Orange City. Laying of railroads in those days was a tremendous undertaking. After every foot of the route was surveyed, bridges were built, hollows filled, and grades raised. The entire roadbed was prepared with scrapers drawn by horses or mules. It was said that mules knew when it was quitting time, and they would no longer work. Overtime benefits didn't interest the stubborn beasts. One of the railroad construction workers came down with the smallpox and started an epidemic of the dread disease. Several of the settlers died, including Mrs. Jelle Pelmulder, little Anthony Betten Jr., Mr. and Mrs. William Jongewaard, and Simon Kuiper, who was Superintendent of Schools.

Pictured below and on the succeeding three pages is a unique photograph showing Central Avenue.

Interior of general store owned by Mr. George Brolsma, father of Mrs. Nic Bogaard. Also in the picture are Minnie Betten (in black) and Mrs. Case Vogelaar. This store was located originally where the E & J store now stands.

Mr. Peter Van Gorp — Harness Shop. One of the first businesses in Orange City.

Home Scenes

Who has not heard parents or grandparents tell stories of their younger days? Families were more closely knit in those days, since survival was a joint family effort. Mother and daughters were kept busy with the many household tasks, and often a hired girl was necessary while the children were young. Father and sons worked side by side in the farming operation. When the boys were small, a hired man was usually employed. He would work in the summer for wages and for room and board in the winter when chores made up most

of the work.

Families were usually large and bustling. A growing, healthy family was never full, so there was always bread to bake. As many as nine big loaves were baked at a time, sometimes three times or more a week. Besides that, cornbread, corn mush, or pancakes were prepared for hearty breakfasts. Then, during the long days of hard work, there were the morning and afternoon lunches to tide the men over to their regular dinner and supper meals.

Every farm family prepared, hoed, and weeded a big garden. The children usually helped with the picking. When picking strawberries, raspberries, gooseberries, blackberries, or currants they would race to see who would have their little pail filled first so they would graduate to a bigger pail. Mother turned the pickings into delicious jams and jellies and stored them in crocks. Plums were made into jam; grapes and apples into jelly. Apples also be-

came sauce or dried apple rings, and some were packed in barrels and stored for the winter in the cellar. When jars were available for canning, many fruits and vegetables were cooked and canned, and then set proudly on shelves in the fruit cellar, ready for the coming winter and spring.

Several members of the family helped with milking the cows. Each had his own cows to milk by hand. While "Bossy" ate hay out of the manger, pails were filled with rich, foamy milk. Memories of the sounds of rhythmic spurts of milk into milk pails still linger in the minds of some Orange City residents. Occasionally "Bossy" had to swat a fly, and her tail would swing in the milker's face. Or she would lift a leg, and, if the pail was not grabbed quickly, the milk bucket would be kicked over — a feast for the cats which usually sat attentively around, purring and waiting for an accident or for their pan to be filled with milk. Usually, the calves were fed and the cows bedded down with nice clean straw before milking time, so the full milk pails were ready to be taken to the house. Before the time of separators, the milk was put in large shallow pans, so the cream would form a layer on the top. After it was skimmed off, the cream was churned into butter in barrel or plunger churns. What a welcomed sound when at last the "clunk-clunk" of the forming chunks of butter was heard. Then the mother would pour off the buttermilk, work the butter with a butter paddle to get the rest of the buttermilk out, salt it, mold it, and decorate the tasty final product with fancy markings made with the paddle. Sometimes butter was traded for groceries. But with the coming of the separator, the cream was hauled away to the cream-

ery by the cream hauler and the old barrel and plunger churns were retired to the attic.

Threshing time meant busy days for men and women alike. Pies and cakes were baked and heaps of food prepared for the lunches and dinners. Sometimes even breakfasts and suppers were served. What feasting it was for the hard-working men, since every housewife served her best and tried to have something that the neighbors had not served. Mrs. Wm. Scholten was the first to serve jello in their threshing ring. When her husband went to town for it, he could not remember the name and said in Dutch he wanted "the stuff that trembled."

Butchering time was a busy time. Some farmers kept fifty-gallon wooden barrels full of brine for curing hams and shoulders. The pork chops and ribs were fried out and put under fat in crocks. Large pieces of beef were cured and smoked for dried beef. Other meat, including steak, was baked in the oven and stored in tallow. When jars were available, much of the meat was canned. Refrigeration was little used, although cutting and hauling ice from nearby rivers was a regular chore after a cold snap each winter.

There was always a lot of sewing to do. In some homes a seamstress would move in for a week at a time to make the fine beautiful dresses which required five to ten yards of material. Many a fine seam was turned by hand in those days.

The wash board was gradually replaced by the washing machine. The machines had a lever attached to the dasher that had to be pulled back and forth. What a tiresome job for children! But some were clever and built a "dog-tread" for power. Then the noise of the gas motor appeared for a while until electricity became available. Water was pumped by hand or windmill from the cistern, heated in a boiler on the stove, and carried to and poured into the machine. Then, after the washing was done, it was carried outside again to be thrown away.

Ironing was done with sad irons heated on the stove. They ironed a stiffly-starched collar and bosom. The high-test gas iron was an improvement that lasted until the appearance of the electric iron.

The old black cookstove always had a kettle of water boiling on it. It was handy when the men came in or a neighbor stopped by for coffee or or when there was a frozen pipe to thaw. It also served as a humidifier. The old black stove was replaced by the prized blue ones, and maybe a "Quick Meal," on a tan and white stove. These improved stoves had a reservoir for heating water, warming ovens above the stove for keeping things warm and a shelf above that where mittens were dried.

The chores for the children included keeping the cob box and wood box filled, gathering the eggs from mean broody hens, feeding the chickens filling water troughs and fountains, and caring for pets. Broody hens were set on nests of eggs in the "brooi bak" (brooding box) for hatching chicks. Each mother hen would care for her own brood when hatched, and if disturbed, she would fly at and attack anything. Few people anymore can picture a mother hen gathering her chicks under her wings. The bright-eyed chicks would then peek out from among the feathers, feeling safe, secure, and warm.

In prosperous times, beautiful and spacious homes were built with attractive furnishings. The base-burner, with its ruddy glowing coals, gave heat day and night. And no fancy house was built without "de beste Kamer" — the parlor. In this congenial atmosphere, company was entertained and daughters took their beaus. Here was the organ around which the family would gather to sing both Dutch and English hymns and the psalms. Many a Gospel Hymnal became well worn in the family parlor, since singing was a popular pastime. Some families formed their own singing groups, and neighborhoods often gathered together to sing and enjoy themselves.

The room enjoyed was the dining room, really the family room. The family would gather around the table to work, study, or read by the light of lamp. The catechism lesson was learned and recited to father or mother. Mother knitted woolen black stockings, scarves, caps, and mittens needed for winter. Some of the children played home-made games, dominoes, or checkers, or looked at the new mail-order and seed catalogues.

Young people got together for sleighing parties, hay-rides, and spelling bees. They also attended boys' and girls' societies and singing school or just visited at the neighbors. Mother and father visited too and discussed the topics of the day, especially religion.

The last and best scene to recall is the family devotions. Before partaking of any meal a blessing was asked. After the meal, a portion of scripture was read, with the older children following in their Bibles and being called on to read verses too. (And oh, if you lost the place!) This was concluded with a thanksgiving prayer. Some families also had other evening devotions.

Old mill referred in history stood on the Wm Rieckhoff property—now the Northwestern College football field.

19

Farming During The First Years

Farm Buildings—John A. Kleinhesselink, 1 mile south and 1 mile west of Orange City

During the first years of the colony, grain was cut with a scythe. An attachment of long, finger-like rods made it possible to lay the cut grain in swaths. In a day of hard labor one man could cut about three acres. Two more men bound the grain into bundles with stems of straw (not twine). With the new horse-drawn reaper, however, eight acres could be mowed per day. The five-foot-wide reaper cut the grain and laid it on a platform, where two men hand-tied it into bundles. (A later binder back cut and bound the grain with twine all in one operation.) The bundles were set up in shocks until they dried. Then the bundles were hauled home in wagons and set into coneshaped stacks. Four stacks usually made up one setting. The first threshing machine had to have the twine cut and the loose straw fed by hand. A sharp blade on a wooden handle, strapped to a man's wrist,

cut the twine. Arie Noteboom lost a finger in this type of operation. At first the threshed grain was sacked and the straw stacked. Later, it was funneled into wagons and scooped into grain bins. Later, still, elevators and blowers replaced the scoop.

The power was furnished by six-horse teams hitched to a staked-down power. The horses would go round and round. Then came the steam-engines. Coal was used to heat the water which created steam. A water boy with a large tank hauled in the water to be converted into steam. A big belt from the steam engine set the thresher separator into motion. Sometimes the threshing season lasted into late fall, with snowflakes flying, before the threshing was finished. Neighbors helped each other by exchanging their labor. Gasoline tractors replaced the steam engine. Combines re-

21

John Roelofs and John Moes plowing on the John A. Kleinhesselink farm

placed the threshing separators, and today most grain is combined in the field and hauled home or to the elevator in motor trucks.

Seeding by hand became a lost art after seeders were invented. The first disks were small - - only six to nine feet wide. Before the disk, seed beds were prepared with cultivators, and shovels threw out corn roots from the previous year's crop. Now with the huge diesel tractors, there is no limit on the size of the disk.

Early corn planters were clumsy. Each field was marked crosswise. Then two men on a planter rode the field lengthwise - - one driving the team, the other dropping the corn kernels at the cross marks. Later, the mechanical planter had wire for cross checking - - two rows at a time. Now four-row and larger planters with fertilizer attachments cover in minutes what it took our pioneers hours to complete.

Corn husking was a long, tedious task. Early in the morning when the stars were still shining, men would be on their way to the field. The men would rip open the husks with a peg attached to their thumbs. The corn would be broken at the shank and tossed into a wagon, one ear at a time. Later, the men used a hook in the palm of their hand instead of the peg. This was the hardest of farm labors. It whetted their appetites. Breakfast usually consisted of pancakes or corn bread or a delicacy for early Hollanders, "vet and stroop" - - bread dipped in bacon grease with a goodly helping of syrup.

Often there was frost on the cornstalks. Mittens became wet and frozen. Most men took fruit jars full of coffee, wrapped in paper, with them to the fields. The coffee with a few slices of home-baked bread gave them a welcomed coffee break. It took half a day to pick a load of corn. Then, the load was scooped from the wagon into a crib which was back-breaking task. This operation was repeated in in the afternoon and consequently, chores had to be done by lantern light. Now cornpicking machines of huge capacity are used for all this labor.

John Roelofs' Threshing Crew

Tractors have replaced "Old Dobbin" on the farm. Some modern tractors are so powerful that it is difficult to comprehend their capacity. However, today's large mechanical horse can never muster up human affections as did the old faithful team of horses. Frank Noteboom can still point to the spot behind his grove where his old faithful team "Jim and Fanny" are buried. True horse power is gone. Now horses are enjoyed only for riding and pleasure.

The method of putting up hay also has undergone a tremendous change. Pioneers pitched hay onto a rack, hauled it home, and pitched it by hand, either onto a stack or into a barn. Later came the slings and then horses pulled the hay into the loft overhead. Much of this is now baled in the field by the fastest method. It is chopped by machine in the field, blown into a covered wagon and preserved in large silos. Now farmers have several tractors and all types of attachments which eliminates almost all hand work. Pioneers cleaned the manure from their barns by tossing it onto a

wagon. What a pitching! Out in the field, the same process was called for, except farmers also had to twist their wrists in order to spread the manure somewhat uniformly. Manure spreaders have changed all that.

Hendrik Top was one of the first to buy a manure spreader. The manure was loaded onto the spreader by hand. His son Gerrit would then drive out into the field, set the beater in action and as the horses walked along, the manure was spread evenly over the field. Neighboring friends kidded Gerrit that he could now do the dirty job wearing his best suit and white collar.

All farming has changed. Wouldn't the pioneers be surprised at the bright yard lights and all the motors and gadgets which can be put into use by a flick of a switch. No more chores in dim lantern light, no more pumping water by hand or dipping with buckets. No more milking by hand (on many farms, no milking at all). Farming for Sioux County farmers, changed drastically when Sioux Electric Cooperative Association came into being.

1890 – 1918

Fire Department Float Fourth of July Celebration 1901

Farmland that had been bought for $7 or $8 an acre now sold for $30 to $40 per acre. Indians no longer camped along the West Branch where they had often held burial ceremonials.

Churches had been organized in Maurice, Middleburg, Newkirk, Sioux Center, Hull, and Alton. The people looked forward to Sunday School picnics and mission fests.

The first board walks were laid. The streets were very muddy when it rained. Charles Sterrenburg remembers dragging the streets with a drag from the livery stable. After a rain, it sometimes took two teams to pull a wagon. There were only kerosene street lights in the main district.

Bicycles appeared and were used for trips as far away as Leota, Minnesota.

The twenty-fifth anniversary of the colony was observed in 1895. The Volksvriend printed a special red-cover edition for the occasion. At the twenty-fifth celebration, the older people recalled experiences suffered in earlier days and were thankful for God's blessings. The young people enjoyed street attractions, lemonade, and ice cream.

The American Church, built in 1888, burned and was replaced with another in 1896.

On July 3, 1897 or 1898, a cyclone ripped off the tin roof of the town hall and carried it a half mile east into the pasture of C. Hospers. The Hospers' home and others were considerably damaged. The next day was the Fourth of July. So, to get away from all the curious spectators, the Hospers' went by carriage to Sioux Center's Independence celebration. While there, the bleachers collapsed where Frank Hospers was sitting.

The present Court House and the jail were voted for and built in 1902. At that time there were several houses, a hotel, a blacksmith shop, a lumberyard, and apple and plum trees on the block where the Court House now stands.

Hotel Betten, Orange City, Iowa

Water Tower, Orange City, Iowa.

Much credit should be given to the doctors who endured many hardships to help the people. They were on call all hours of the day and with their faithful drivers would make house calls in all kinds of weather. How were doctors summoned to a farm? When a new baby was expected, for example, an arrangement was made with a neighbor to fetch the doctor. The expectant father would tap on his neighbor's window and his friend would quickly harness the team or saddle the horse and be off to get the doctor. Then the doctor and his driver, with fresh team of horses, would sometimes beat the farmer back, who now took it slower.

There was no hospital where surgery was performed. One night Dr. Jepson of Sioux City and Dr. Wormser performed an appendectomy on a kitchen table under the light of a big lamp borrowed from a church. Many pans of boiling water were kept ready for sterilizing instruments. The operation was successful, and the patient, Anna Noteboom, later Mrs. Gerrit Bloemendaal, recovered.

The first telephones were installed in the first decade of the twentieth century. Farmers along the telephone route were each responsible for a certain distance. Farmers drove their wagons into town, loaded up the huge telephone poles, and distributed them at uniform intervals in each mile.

The First Automobiles

Most of the first automobiles operated on one or two-cylinder motors, with a stick drive steering device. This stick looked like an upside-down 'L' at the top of the steering post. Many autos had high buggy wheels with a radius of three to four feet. A later model had a four-cylinder motor, a regular steering wheel instead of a stick, and small wheels In some cars the only way to get into the back seat was through a door at the rear. Often wives rode in the back seat.

Some of Orange City's early car owners include:

Mayor H. Slikkerveer, single cylinder, stick steering and no top. Believed to have been an Oldsmobile;

Arie Vander Meide, a single cylinder Cadillac;

Dr. A. De Bey, a Flanders Roadster with steering wheel and small wheels. It had no top. Rumors are that he had difficulty getting behind the steering wheel.

Ring Jasper, a high buggy-type wheel International with chain drive. It was a two cylinder and made so much noise that he could be heard coming at some distance.

A 1912 Cadillac owned by William Reickhoff. Pictured - Chauffeur — Mr. Gerrit Kempers, Reickhoff children and two maids — Emma and Dora Hykstra

1915 Ford Sedan — Note Sioux County License 85-828 Pictured Bob De Haan

Boland — Duven Garage — Located just South of Dr. Osdoba Dentist office — now vacant lot.
Year 1919
Pictured from left to right — Mr. Henry Boland, Cornie Den Hartog, James Duven, Henry Den Hartog, John Den Hartog and Jerry Kraai.

First Automobile Fatality

Mr. E. H. Casjens drove a four-cylinder Chalmers regular steering wheel, and small tires. On October 5, 1912, Mr. and Mrs. Casjens were driving in the vicinity of Maurice. At the east edge of Maurice Mr. Casjens came upon a deep mudhole in the dirt road. He shifted into intermediate gear before attempting to cross. Somehow, the car upset and rolled down a steep grade. Mrs. Casjens was sitting alone in the back seat. The top was down. She was thrown clear of the car, but Mr. Casjens was pinned beneath the steering wheel. He was taken to the home of James De Jong (Harold's father) where Dr. Oggel, who was practicing physician in Maurice, treated him. Mr. Casjens died fourteen hours later. He was the first auto fatality in Orange City, probably in Sioux County. Some people think it was the first fatality in Northwest Iowa.

Last Train Ride

Inconvenience is perhaps the term most applicable to Orange City's passenger train service. The city apparently was built to the north of the Chicago and Northwestern Railroad tracks with main street about one mile from the station. When railways began to discontinue their passenger trains, Orange City's passenger service was one of the first to go. Many citizens took the last train ride on the line from Orange City to Hawarden and back.

Church Language Problems

During World War I, services in the Orange City and area churches were still being conducted in the langauge of Holland. Patriotism ran high; ministers were forced to follow their usual Dutch sermon, with a brief translation into English. The younger people, however, wanted the services to be spoken entirely in English, to the extent that a group separated from the First Reformed Church and organized Trinity Reformed Church in 1919. A similar situation existed in the First Christian Reformed Church, and in 1921, the Second Christian Reformed Church came into being. Soon the two mother churches also adopted English services.

Also during World War I, prices were highly inflated. Land skyrocketed to $400 and even as high as $1,000 per acre. Rumors circulated that if you didn't buy a farm right then, you might never have a farm home of your own. Many farms also were purchased from a speculative motive. Farm commodity prices were high; corn went up to $2 per bushel.

Armistice was signed on November 11, 1918, and about two years later prices dropped. Financial difficulties set in and continued through the 1920's with the great stock market crash in 1929. Many families lost farms, homes, and personal property—in many cases their entire life's savings.

Adding to the peoples' miseries were the drought and dust storms of the late twenties and early thrities. Dust blew from the dried plowed fields forming huge dust drifts, much like the snow drifts of winter's blizzards.

Then came the never-to-be-forgotten winter of 1936. It snowed so much that roads were impassable for days at a time. Many streets in Orange City could not be traveled on for several weeks. February, alone, recorded five huge blizzards. Temperatures dipped to 20 and 30 degrees below zero every morning. For 35 consecutive days the thermometer never registered higher than zero.

With all the moisture from the melting snow as a reserve, bumper crops seemed an almost certianty.

Corn never looked more beautiful and promising than that year. And then like the frigid weather of the previous winter, came the extreme heat. Temperatures soared in excess of 100 degrees day after day with no rains to refresh the parched earth or the wilting corn. A more complete crop failure occurred that year than Sioux County had or has ever experienced.

A Sad Drowning Tragedy

Seldom is a community plunged into such overwhelming sorrow as it was on Saturday, July 14, 1934, when word came that five Orange City girls had lost their lives while swimming in Lake West Okoboji.

Dead were:

MARGARET BLACKBURN, 28, Davenport, Iowa—chaperon and instructor at Northwestern Junior College and Academy.

WILMYNA MUILENBURG, 18, daughter of Mrs. Jennie Muilenburg.

VERA MUILENBURG, 17, Wilmyna's sister.

ELSIE HERWYNEN, 19, daughter of Mr. and Mrs. Isaac Herwynen.

WILMA DUIMSTRA, 19, daughter of Mr. and Mrs. F. D. Duimstra.

The tragedy occurred shortly before noon while the girls, together with Miss Eleanor Rozeboom, 16, daughter of Mr. and Mrs. H. H. Rozeboom, and Mildred Vanden Bos, 18, daughter of Mr. and Mrs. W. W. Vanden Bos, were bathing off Pillsbury Point at Lake Okoboji.

The young ladies, with Miss Blackburn as chaperon, had left Friday morning for a week's outing at the lakes. On Saturday morning the girls donned their bathing attire in preparation for a little dip in the lake. All were having great fun, laughing, giggling, and splashing and about ready to go in for lunch when one of the girls slipped off a wet, moss-covered rock into deep water. In a brief moment panic set in.

Eleanor, Mildred, and Miss Blackburn, all good swimmers, hurried to the rescue of those in distress. When almost exhausted, Miss Blackburn told Eleanor and Mildred to hurry to the shore for help. Eleanor made it to shore to give the alarm; Mildred, totally exhausted, dropped onto a rock but fortunately her head was above water. Miss Blackburn lost her life in further rescue attempts. Their screams brought vacationers running from all directions. Ralph Luchinger of Milaca, Minnesota, was fishing nearby. He and Henry Shutt of Omaha, Nebraska, and Russel Rute of Spencer, Iowa, rowed to the spot where the girls had gone down. They were successful in recovering two of the bodies. Leo Jolin of Sioux City, Iowa, brought in a third body. Divers recovered the two remaining bodies. Miss Blackburn's body was taken to Davenport. She had spent four years teaching French, Latin, and Physical Education at Northwestern. She had so many friends in Orange City that she was considered to be an Orange Citian.

A mass funeral service was held on Tuesday afternoon, July 17, 1934, for the four Orange City girls from the First Reformed Church. Some 5,000 people attended. Seats and loud speakers were arranged on the church lawn. The Rev. Jacob Heemstra, college president, the Rev. Bert Brower, the Rev. J. G. Brower, the Rev. R. Bronkema, and the Rev. Gerrit Pennings officiated at the services. Services for Miss Margaret Blackburn were held in Davenport at the same hour as the services for the four girls in Orange City. About 35 Northwestern students traveled to Davenport to pay last respects.

A sobering sight was four hearses abreast, bearing the bodies of the four Orange City victims, traveling slowly north on Central Avenue toward First Reformed Church. In addition to the four cars bearing the pall bearers, 111 cars made up the funeral procession. It was 6 P.M. when the last person had filed by the caskets. The procession then continued to West Lawn cemetery for the burial service. Indeed, it was the end of a sad, sad day in Orange City.

The two survivors were Miss Eleanor Rozeboom, now Mrs. Eugene Schula of Albuquerque, New Mexico, and Miss Mildred Vanden Bos, now Mrs. Rev. Benjamin Ver Steeg of California.

Tornadoes

Tornadoes have plagued Sioux County from time to time. Even shortly after colonization when the pioneers did not know much about tornadoes, one caused destruction and loss of life. It is not possible to give a full account of each tornado; they will be referred to only briefly.

June 14, 1914, about 5 P.M. a tornado swooped down and totally destroyed the Allen farm a few miles southwest of Hospers. It caused further damage east of Hospers.

The tornado of June 16, 1944, caused perhaps the most widespread destruction. Roaring in from South Dakota, it first spent its rages west of Sioux Center. Then it swooped through five farms northwest of Orange City, and again east of Orange City into the Hospers area. A total of 79 farms were touched and 35 were totally demolished. The

miracle is that not one life was lost.

The City of Orange City will long remember Sunday, September 22, 1968, when late afternoon a tornado hit the south edge of the city, and with hardly any warning, cut a path along the west edge of the city to the northwest leaving streets cluttered with trees and debris. All power was cut off, and a night of complete darkness followed. Never will Orange Citians forget the next day, Monday, when farmers and many neighboring townfolk converged upon the city and helped with the fastest clean-up ever witnessed. (Turn to the story of the Orange City Volunteer Firemen elsewhere in this book for a tornado alert system which resulted from the 1968 tornado.)

Flood

September 17, 1926, will be remembered as the date of the great flood, referring to the high waters at the Million Dollar Corner six miles west of Orange City. Dark clouds formed about noon, and rain poured down in torrents most of the afternoon and into the night. An area church conference was in progress at Sioux Center, and many participants were forced to remain there for the night, because the flood had washed out several bridges. Mrs. Sip Terpstra of Hospers had left for the conference in the morning. Her husband, a jeweler at Hospers, and the couples' young son were to pick her up that evening. Business had brought Mr. Terpstra to Orange City, and he and his son continued from here to Sioux Center. When he arrived at the Million Dollar Corner, the road already was covered with water for about a half mile north. A huge wall of water stopped the motor of his automobile. He and his young son climbed on top of the car. Some spectators near the corner spotted them when the lightning flashed but were unable to reach father and son. The body of the young boy was found the following day. Searching parties worked for days, but Mr. Terpstra's body was not discovered for two weeks.

The western part of the County suffered the most damage from the flood. Several others lost their lives. In the city of Hawarden waters from Dry Creek ran rampart through the streets.

Another flood with its horrible memories happened Sunday, June 7, 1953, when from eight to twelve inches of rain fell over a wide area. Streams and creeks emptied into the Floyd River which on Monday converged on Sioux City, Iowa, doing damage the likes of which Sioux City has never known. Fourteen Sioux Citians lost their lives.

A Musical and Talented Town

Chimes of Normandy — Musical Comedy rendered by Orange City Talent Friday Evening, May 20, 1910. Musical Director - Prof. G. J. Dinkeloo Pianist — Miss Magdalene Synhorst.

The first brass band was organized by C. Hospers in 1876. Members were Tom Dunham, Jacob Betten, Gerrit Bolks, Henry Ten Broek, Frank Le Cocq, Tiete Pool, John Vande Steeg, Henry Slikkeveer, C. Hospers, and Prof. Smead.

Some remembered programs and concerts are the following:

In 1909— Olde Folkes Concert

In 1910— The Chimes of Normandy

In 1920— The Golden Jubilee Pageant by Judson Kolyn. This was given in commeration of the 50th Anniversary of the founding of the Orange City Colony.

In 1919— Philharmonic Orchestra of Orange City —directed by Prof. Frederick Wick gave a program.

The Orange City Choral Society directed by Mrs. Marian Hospers gave Handel's "Messiah" at least two times.

Hiawatha—given by the Orange City Choral Society directed by Mrs. Marian Hospers, in a joint concert with the Sioux City Symphony, conducted by Leo Kucinski.

Beginning with May, 1936, the Tulip Festival has been held annually. The townspeople always delight packed-house audiences for three nights with musicals or operettas, such as "Red Mill," "Sweethearts," "The Sound of Music," and many others.

Northwestern College, the high schools, the grade schools, and the churches all present concerts, plays, and programs that bring forth the wonderful talent with which we as a community are blest.

OLIVER!

Community Living

Located in the calm surroundings of the rural Midwest, Orange City has much to offer as a place to live—small enough to enjoy a neighborly friendship—large enough to supply an urban touch.

In keeping with Dutch tradition, its people take pride in their well-kept homes, lawns, streets, and commercial areas.

A double system of public and private schools from kindergarten through high school, new and modern buildings and equipment, highly-qualified faculties, promise a high standard of education. Northwestern College augments this with a complete four-year college program. Hardly could a small community hope for better educational opportunities for their children and youth. Flowing forth from all this are the benefits of athletic entertainment, music, drama, and art.

One of the annual highlights of Orange City's living is the Tulip Festival. Not only is the Festival an exciting time in itself, but preparing for it proves even more exciting. The young ladies are selected as nominees for Queen. In regular election the number is the symbolic seven.

Then amidst gay pageantry, providing a full evening's entertainment, the Festival Queen is named. The final climax comes when on each Festival day she is adorned with the crown of Festival reign in a colorful coronation ceremony. For the young ladies this certainly is an important part of Orange City's community life.

The early settlers held the spiritual in high regard. The city's seven churches stand as a tribute to these pioneers, but a greater tribute to them is that the generations have sustained those beliefs. Over the century, this influence has reached far beyond the congregational confines. Only the Church holds hope and promise for the future.

Mr. and Mrs. Arie Vander Meide
(taken on their 50th wedding anniversary)

Mr. and Mrs. Arie Vander Meide
(taken on their 50th wedding anniversary)

Mr. Arie Vander Meide was born November 27, 1852 at Pella, Iowa, son of Jacob Vander Meide and Jannetje Groenveld. He married Gysbertje Pas on March 21, 1871 at Pella, Iowa. Early in the spring of 1870 Mr. Vander Meide homesteaded the farm two miles north and one and three fourth miles west of Orange City. The family soon moved to Orange City where Mr. Vander Meide was active in civic affairs. In 1889 he was elected Mayor of Orange City and in 1891 he became a member of the Vander Meide & Lohr Loan Company. He was a cashier at the Northwestern State Bank in 1895 where he also served as a director. He was an active member of the American Reformed Church and served as a deacon for several terms. He was one of the first Supervisors of Sioux County. Their golden wedding was celebrated on March 21, 1921 at their home west of the Sioux County Capital building.

The Family Album

Mr. and Mrs. Sjoerd De Groot and family — Mr. De Groot was born in the Netherlands and came to this country in the year 1875. Mrs. De Groot was born in Virginia, then came to Pella, Iowa. They farmed north of Orange City, Iowa, buying the land for $8.00 an acre. Their children—Mrs. Ben Ter Hark (deceased), Peter (died at the age of 19), Louis (deceased), and John S. De Groot who resides on the farm a half mile east of Northwestern College.

Mrs. William Rieckhoff coming and going

Pictured above is the first Orange City fire department formed in 1897. Left to right, front row: Henry Dykstra, R. De Cook, Herman Nieuwenhof, George Pas and Henry Ver Schoor. Back row: Ike Herwynen, Isaac Vos, Jake Ypma, John Behrend, Herman Totts, John Brink, Fred Michel and John Eerkes. Dick De Cook was the last member to die. His funeral was held recently.

Dentist Office — above De Haan Electric

Mr. and Mrs. Gerrit Jan Hofmeyer

Mr. and Mrs. Hofmeyer were born in the Netherlands and set out for the new world in 1871. After an 18 month stay in Chicago they traveled on to northwest Iowa arriving in Alton, Iowa in December 1872. They obtained a homestead in the Orange City area and started farming In later years they retired and became Orange City residents.

Pictured left to right — Mr. and Mrs. Herman Hofmeyer, Mr. and Mrs. Gerrit J. Hofmeyer, Mr. and Mrs. J. W. Hofmeyer. These brothers and wives all celebrated their 50th wedding anniversaries.

Children of Mr. and Mrs. William Hospers

Left to right — Wm Hospers, Jake Hospers, Mae (Mrs. A. J. Kolyn).

Mr. and Mrs. Frank De Haan

Mr. De Haan was born on November 18, 1858. Mrs. De Haan was born on October 26, 1868. They farmed in the Orange City vicinity.

Funeral Procession

Funeral of Mrs. Hiltje Brower grandmother of Mrs. Chris Aalberts and Mrs. Henry Haarsma. Approximately 1889. Two ministers and the driver are in the first buggy. The First Reformed Church is in the background.

Jacob Cleveringa Family—Back row, left to right: Kate (Mrs. Herman Bartman), Ralph, Abe, Alice (Mrs. Ralph Bloemendaal). Second row: Gerb, Mr. and Mrs. Jacob Cleveringa, Nick. Front row: Coba (Mrs. Gerrit Boone), Cornelia (Mrs. Henry Roghair).

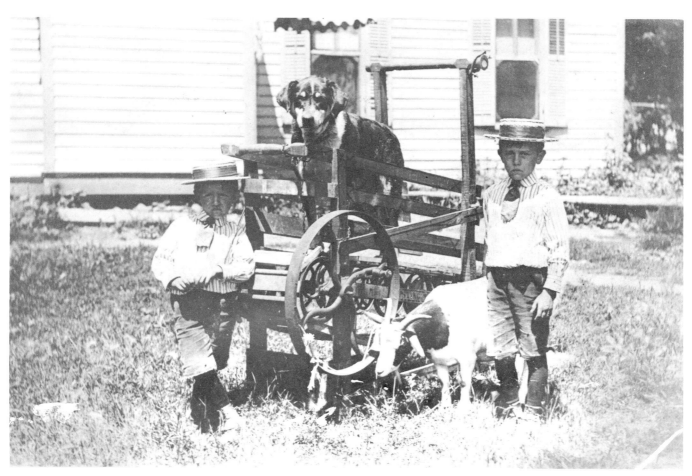

This is a picture of the tread mill power used for washing machine. If the dog was not available the goat was also trained to do this. If neither one was available then the two young boys — namely Raymond and Harry De Jong were called on.

This picture was taken on the farm of Mr. P. G. De Jong South of Orange City now owned by Mr. Harry De Jong.

Mr. and Mrs. Henry Muyskens and their children, Jennie (Mrs. McKee) and Henry taken in 1900. Mr. Muyskens was the first harness maker in Orange City.

The John Vande Steeg Family—Seated front row, left to right: Mrs. Vande Steeg, Dorothy (Hanser), Mr. Vande Steeg. Second row: George, Jacoba (Kilgore), Florence (Granger), Mae, Arthur. Back row: Lucille.

John Vande Steeg was born in Pella, Iowa in December, 1861, son fo Mr. and Mrs. Gerrit Vande Steeg. When he was a young boy he came with his father and family to Sioux County. He taught school for a short time in 1870-71. He resigned and went into the mercantile business which he held throughout his life. John Vande Steeg and Mary Pas were married on March 25, 1881. Mr. Vande Steeg was interested in music—played in the band and sang in different organizations. He was active in the community and particpated in civic projects. He died in May, 1914.

Mr. and Mrs. W. Short

Wells S. Short was born in 1865 in Honeye, New York. He was a son of Spencer D. Short and Lorinda Pitts. He came to Orange City at the age of 18 and became book-keeper at Northwestern State Bank. Except for 4 years spent in McIntosch, Minnesota at the First National Bank, he devoted his entire life to banking at Northwestern State Bank, becoming its president in 1905. He retired as president in 1945 but served as Chairman of the Board until his death in 1951, thus serving this institution for 67 years out of a life span of 86 years. Under his capable leadership and strenuous efforts this bank was able to qualify as one of the select banks in Iowa which was able to pay its depositors 100 cents on the dollar in the depression of the 30's. He was married to Johanna De Jong, daughter of Hendrick De Jong, a Sioux County pioneer.

Mr. and Mrs. Hein Rowenhorst

Rowenhorst Brothers and Sisters

Front row left to right — Mrs. Hendrika Mouw, Mrs. Christina Braskamp, back row Albert Rowenhorst, Hein Rowenhorst.

Business Street, Orange City, Iowa.

CORNER THIRD AND WASHINGTON ST., ORANGE CITY, IA.
(Publ. for De ..ruif & Lubbers.)

WASHINGTON STREET ORANGE CITY, IA. 652

No.1.
DeKruif & Lubbers.
Washington St.
ORANGE CITY, IA
DABBS Photo.

Mr. and Mrs. Peter Mouw and daughter Anna
(Mrs. Steve De Jong)

Mr. and Mrs. Peter Mouw played an important part in Orange City's past century of development.

Mr. Mouw was born in the Netherlands in 1852 and emigrated with his parents to Pennsylvania in 1866. In 1868 they trecked to the Iowa prairies settling north of Orange City.

He later married Betsy Koster, daughter of Mr. and Mrs. Jacob Koster of Sioux Center, Iowa, also listed as one of the early pioneer families. He purchased an eighty acre farm one mile North of Orange City at eight dollars an acre. This has since remained the family farm and it is today operated by his grandson, Bernard De Jong.

Mr. Mouw became one of Northwest Iowa's most successful stockmen. As early as 1886 he entered into the business of raising Purebred Hereford Cattle and what latter became known as the Big Type Poland China Hogs. The largest hog he ever raised weighed in excess of 1000 lbs. He exhibited at many fairs, including the World's Fair in Chicago, Iowa and Illinois State Fairs, International Livestock Shows and the World's Fair in St. Louis.

Mr. and Mrs. Mouw remained on this farm until their death and contributed much to the promotion and development of this community. They were active in many church and civic interests.

Packard & 12⁰ E. Main St.

Mr. and Mrs. Tjeerd Heemstra

Mr. Tjeerd Heemstra was born November 8, 1824 at Marrum, Friesland, Netherlands. On March 19, 1846 he was joined in marriage to Syke Hoekstra. The following year the couple emigrated to America and settled near Holland, Michigan where they lived for twenty three years. Convinced that the West offered better opportunities, he joined the movement to Sioux County and arrived in the early spring of 1870, being the first to erect his shanty on the homestead a mile South of Orange City. A part of his farm is now incorporated as Industrial Air Park Subdivision. Mr. Heemstra held various positions of responsibility in the church and community. He died at Orange City, Iowa April 13, 1901.

Mr. Henry Hospers

Mr. William Hospers

Mr. Cornelius Hospers

Henry, Cornelius and William Hospers were brothers. All were leading citizens. Henry is referred to often in the history story. Cornelius and William were merchants who operated a general store where the Northwestern State Bank sits now. Mr. and Mrs. Cornelius Hospers in their wedding dress in 1879 show a little of the spark in those days. The latter were parents of Mrs. G. J. Slobe who is still living in Orange City.

Mr. and Mrs. John T. Klein and Mr. and Mrs. Albert Smeenk operated the Fair Store around the turn of the century where the Korver 5 & 10 is now located. Mrs. Klein and Mrs. Smeenk were daughters of Henry Hospers.

Mr. and Mrs. Cornelius Hospers

Mr. and Mrs. John T. Klein

Mr. and Mrs. Albert Smeenk

The Bloemendaal Brothers — Left to right — John, Ralph, Gerrit, Henry, Joe, Jim, William. Two of these are living today. Henry and William.

Inside of the Bakery

Sam Van Vliet, at the left, is the baker; P. De Vries, center, is decorating a wedding cake; Bastiaan Vander Aarde is standing near the brick oven. The picture was taken in 1902.

Mr. and Mrs. Bastiaan Vander Aarde sr.

Bastiaan and Agatha Vander Aarde sr. and children Klaas, Pieter, Aafje (Mrs. Jake Borgman sr.) Anne, Trynke, Bastiaan jr. migrated to America from the Netherlands in 1874 and came to Orange City. They bought the 80 acres just southeast of Orange City known as the Vander Aarde addition. Their occupation was mostly farming and dairy business. In 1890 a brick factory was started, located just north of the Chicago and Northwestern railroad tracks on the Vander Aarde addition. Bastiaan jr. also worked in this new business. The only remaining house of these bricks is owned by Northwestern College today. In 1896 it was forced out of business because of the depression. Two children born in Orange City are Elizabeth (Mrs. Herman TePaske) and Gerrit.

Mr. and Mrs. Henry De Groot

Mrs. De Groot, Jennie Roetman, born October 28, 1871 came to the United States from the Netherlands with her parents, Mr. and Mrs. Gerrit Roetman in 1882, at the age of eleven years.

Henry De Groot, born in the Netherlands February 13, 1865, came to this country in 1885. In 1887 he purchased a prairie homestead in Capel Township, the deed to the land coming directly from the Governor of Iowa. He broke the prairie and started putting the land into production, and on March 20, 1890 brought his bride to their new two room farm home.

Always very active in church and community work, Mr. De Groot after retiring in 1920 took up various responsibilities in the Orange City area and served as Treasurer of Northwestern Classical Academy and Northwestern Junior College for over twenty years.

Mrs. De Groot passed away in March, 1933 and Mr. De Groot died in December, 1946.

Mae Vande Steeg

Mae Vande Steeg was born in Orange City, Iowa on December 17, 1884, the daughter of Mr. and Mrs. John Vande Steeg. After graduation from high school, Mae attended the State University of Iowa at Iowa City.

Mae was always interested in the mercantile business, so worked in her father's store until his death in 1912. At that time Mae and her brother Arthur bought the mercantile business from the family estate. She retired from the business in the fall of 1850. She was interested in music, active in the church and interested in the activities of the college. She participated in many civic projects. Mae died on November 5, 1953.

Mr. and Mrs. Jan G. Reinders

Mr. and Mrs. Reinders with their seven sons left Wageningen, Holland in February, 1882. In 1887 they started farming and soon owned their own farm, today owned and operated by two of their grandsons, John B. and Bernard Reinders.

Mr. and Mrs. Pieter Haarsma

Mr. and Mrs. Haarsma came to America in 1893. He was one of the first barbers, having a barber shop and shoe repair shop just west of the city park. Shaves were 5 cents and haircuts 10 cents.

Mr. and Mrs. Arend J. Pennings

Arend J. Pennings left the Netherlands in 1868, was shipwrecked enroute but eventually arrived in America in that year, establishing himself first in the vicinity of Green-leafton, Minnesota. In approximately 1874 he settled in the vicinity of Orange City, Iowa where he lived to the day of his death. The so-called Pennings farm is one mile West and two and one half miles South of Orange City.

From left to right — Gerrit J. (missionary to Arabia), Mr. A. J. Pennings, Gertrude (Mrs. H. I. Muilenberg), Mrs. Pennings, William, Henry.

Four Generations of the Klein Bekman family

Mr. John K. Bekman, sr., Mr. John Albert K. Bekman
Mr. Henry K. Bekman and Mr. Leo Bekman.

Arie Noteboom Family

Mary (Mrs. Cleveringa), Nick, Anna (Mrs. Gerrit Bloemendaal), front row left to right - Mrs. Noteboom, Gerrit, Peter, Frank, Mr. Noteboom.

Business of Vander Aarde and De Vries

Sam Van Vliet, at left, at the soda fountain (first soda fountain in Orange City); Bastiaan Vander Aarde at the rear of the store; Peter De Vries in the center; and George Haverdink at the right. The picture was taken in 1902.

The Church is Built

In the spring of 1871 the First Reformed Church was organized, and its meetings were held in the Public School. On Sunday, part of a partition had to be removed to provide sufficient room for the service. With roughly-made benches as pews, the congregation sat around a stove facing the minister, who preached from a table and chair. Although a few of the early settlers had buggies, many came to church in wagons or on horseback, and quite a few walked so as to give their horses some rest from the hard weeks work of breaking prairie. Lunches were often carried by those living at a distance.

The Christian Reformed Church was organized soon afterwards, with its first permanent building located just east of where the cemetery is now.

Rev. Seine Bolks was called to serve as pastor of the early Reformed Church. He moved to Orange City in the spring of 1872. He and his congregation in the Netherlands had emigrated in 1847 and founded a colony in Overisel, Michigan. Anticipating the potential hardships of isolated frontier life, the Reverend, sometimes known as Father Bolks, had also studied medicine. His experience made him a right servant of God for the struggling pioneers in the trying years which followed. His simple faith, his ministry to the sick, and his over-all counsel were greatly appreciated. He also preached to distant groups during the week.

The Churches of Orange City

In the words of a familiar hymn, "Crowns and thrones may perish, Kingdoms rise and wane, But the Church of Jesus - - Constant will remain!"

And so it has been that through the ages the church has continued; today, it remains firmly established in Orange City as the focal point of community life and activity. Orange Citians are, on the whole, a religious people; and their faith is one which finds expression in worship, acts of benevolence and mercy, Christian missions and education, diligence in work, neighborliness and friendliness, and in numerous other ways.

There are presently seven fully organized churches in Orange City, with an eighth just recently organized. These together represent five different denominational groups — The Reformed Church in America, the Christian Reformed Church, The Christian Missionary Alliance, the Assemblies of God, and the Lutheran Church (Missouri Synod). The two Reformed denominations encompass the majority of the people as might be expected in view of the town's historic and religious heritage.

Most of the settlers of Orange City were of Dutch descent, either offspring of immigrants who had seceded from the State Church in the Netherlands (the Hervormde Kerk) or some who came directly to this country from that Secessionist group. The founders of Orange City came from the Pella area and took with them their familiar ecclesiastical institutions - - notably the Reformed Church which grew rapidly in the Sioux County area, and the relatively new Christian Reformed Church which was destined to play a large role here. Both of these churches have a strongly Calvinistic heritage and claim the Belgic Confession, the Canons of the Synod of Dort, and the Heidelberg Catechism as their Confessional standards. In the Midwest at least, both churches stand in the tradition of the 19th century Secessionst (the "Afscheiding") movement in the Netherlands which emphasized Calvinistic orthodoxy and piety and objected to governmental limitations upon their churches and schools.

Otto Rowenhorst, cabinet maker and carpenter for the Queen of the Netherlands, and Christina his wife was in the Queen's court. They migrated from the Netherlands to America with nine children, Klaas, Myntje, Christina, Giertje, Marinus, Johanna, Albert, Matilda and Hein. Their destination was Waupun, Wisconsin. From there they came to Sioux County and were early Pioneers, homesteading five miles south and two miles west of Orange City. In 1873 they sold this farm to Pieter Hooiveld and then moved two and one-half miles north of Orange City. In 1875 Otto Rowenhorst and three sons, Klaas, Marinus and Hein were the contractors for building of the First Reformed Church. Total contract price for the labor was $1200.00. All of the children were married and lived at various places in Sioux County.

The Dutch Reformed Church had long existed in America, having been established in very early colonial days in the New York - New Jersey area; and most of the 19th century Dutch immigrants to the Midwest affiliated themselves with this firmly established American denomination. Some of the newcomers, however, fearful of the "liberal" influences of the American scene and church and mindful of their experiences in the Netherlands, desired to maintain an independent existence and organized the Christian Reformed Church in Michigan in 1857.

In Orange City the two mother churches—the First Reformed and the First Christian Reformed - - gave birth to a number of daughter congregations. The American Reformed and Trinity Reformed were largely offshoots of the First Reformed Church while the Second Christian Reformed drew its membership largely from the First Christian Reformed Church. Though other factors were involved, the catalytic agent was language; the two older churches were slow to drop the Dutch language in their services and educational efforts.

The Dover Alliance Church and the Assembly of God Church represent more recent additions to the Orange City church scene; and probably reflect somewhat the American "revivalist" influence with its evangelistic and baptistic emphases. These, together with the newly organized Missouri Synod Lutheran Church, also reflect a new element of diversity appearing on the Orange City scene as the community grows and loses some of its homogeneous character. The older churches, too, have become more conscious of their Christian mission in the larger world and are moving out of the cultural milieu which formed them and often bound them to that which was traditional (i.e., Dutch and "Old World").

The Orange City Churches, in spite of the differences that do exist, do stand as a community of believers, united in their common acceptance of the Sovereignty of God and the Lordship of Jesus Christ and desire to share that faith with all who will receive it.

First Reformed Church

The First Reformed Church of Orange City was officially organized on May 6, 1871. Rev. N. Williamson of Illinois, Rev. Peter De Pree of Pella, and elder, W. Gesman of Pella served as the committee on organization. The congregation at the time of organization was composed of thrity-four communicant charter members. They elected the following to serve on the first consistory: Elders: Tjeerd Heemstra, Maarten Verhuel, and Gerrit Vande Steeg Sr., Deacons: Walter Van Rooyen, Sjoerd Sipma, and Jelle Pelmulder. When these men were installed the church observed its first communion service.

The congregation called Rev. Seine Bolks to be their first pastor. He served First Reformed Church from 1872 to 1878. Other ministers who were called to serve this congregation and their years of service are as follows: Rev. Ale Buurma (1879-1889), Rev. H. Vander Ploeg (1890-1893), Dr. Matthew Kolyn (1893-1898), Dr. N. M. Steffens (1898-1901), Rev. E. W. Stapelkamp (1901-(1907), Rev. John Engelsman (1908-1925), Dr. Henry Colenbrander (1925 - 1960), Dr. Raymond Van Heukelom (1961 - present), Rev. Robert Bast, associate pastor (1964 - 1967), Rev. Alvin Eissens, associate pastor (1968 - present).

Worship services were first held in the school house located at that time in the west part of Orange City. The present church building was erected in the year 1874 by Mr. Otto Rouwenhorst. In 1894 the right and left wings were added to the building by Mr. H. De Gooyer. As the congregation grew, still more space was needed and and as a result the church parlor was added in 1913 and the balcony renewed and enlarged in 1926. New windows and doors and modern facilities were also installed at the latter date. The church chapel was added in 1937 so that adequate space would be available for the growing Sunday School and Christian Endeavor groups. The church parlor was also enlarged at this time. The present educational unit was constructed in 1963 to provide office area for the two pastors, house the church library, give additional space for Sunday School, RCYF, and Consistory meetings, as well as Couples Club and various women's organizations.

The First Reformed Church has had the privilege of sharing in the organization of several other Reformed Churches in the nearby area. The

The First Church erected in Orange City still serves as a House of worship.

name of each new church, the date it was organized and the number of communicant members from First Reformed church who united with each new church are: Alton Reformed Church, 1877, 27; First Reformed of Sioux Center, 1877, 26; Newkirk Reformed Church, 1882, 26; First Reformed of Maurice, 1884, 25; Free Grace Reformed of Middleburg, 1885, 29; American Reformed of Orange City, 1885, 13; Trinity Reformed of Orange City, 1919, 55.

At the present time the membership of the congregation numbers 455 families, 965 communicant members, 424 baptized members for a total individual membership of 1389.

In 1908 the congregation experienced the joy of ordaining one of her sons, Gerrit J. Pennings, as Minister of the Word. His call was to the mission field of Arabia and the congregation accepted full responsibility for his support as their first missionary. Since that time the congregation has had the rich blessing of seeing 57 of her sons and daughters enter into full-time Christian service.

The congregation will be celebrating its centennial year, the Lord willing, in 1971, with special services being planned for the first week in May. A more detailed history along with a centennial book will be published at that time.

Educational Wing erected in 1963

Dr. and Mrs. Henry Colenbrander - 1925-1960

First Reformed Church Consistory 1970

Seated—Left to right: John Van Binsbergen, William Schalekamp, 2nd vice-president; Dr. Raymond Van Heukelom, Pastor; Rev. Alvin J. Eissens, Associate Pastor; Robert Hubregtse, clerk; Clifford Mouw.

Standing—Left to right: John De Beer, Melvin Van Peursem, Fred Vander Weerd, Henry G. Huitink, Norman Boonstra, Harold Paekel, Jack Vander Wilt. Frank De Vries, Fred De Beer, Barney Zigtema, Delbert De Haan, Chairman of Deacons; Simon Harmelink, Clifford Oolman, Henry J. Jonker, Howard Hop, Benevolent Treasurer; Willard Rowenhorst, Gerald Jong-erius, Building Fund Treasurer; William H. Kosters, Carl Pennings.   Missing—Gillis Haverdink.

First Christian Reformed Church

The First Christian Reformed Church of Orange City, Iowa was organized on July 14, 1871. The newly organized congregation included ten families and four single persons for a total of ninety six members, twenty four of whom were members in full communion.

The first consistory consisted of four men, namely: Elders; L. Vander Meer, and L. Mars; Deacons: P. Vander Zalm and G. De Zeeuw.

From 1871 until 1885 the congregation met in a small building located in the northwest part of Orange City, Iowa. In 1885 the first part of our present church building was erected at its present location, the pulpit being at the West end thereof.

When the facilities for the growing congregation were no longer adequate, in 1896, the South wing was added to the church building and a pipe organ was installed in 1906.

In the year 1909 the present parsonage was built the consistory room was enlarged and new pews were furnished for the church auditorium. Our church continued to grow and in 1917 the galleries

The First Christian Reformed Church 1885-1896.

were installed to accommodate the increased attendance at the worship services.

The official language used in our church was Dutch, but in the years 1924 to 1929 the English language was introduced into the Sunday School and catechism classes and some evening worship services. On May 11, 1953 the congregation approved a plan to build a full basement, complete with auditorium, classrooms, consistory room, kitchen, heating system, and other facilities to meet the growing demand for more room to conduct the affairs of the church and its various organizations. A plan to completely remodel the superstructure of the church building was approved at a congregational meeting held on December 5, 1960. The entire project, including pews and an Allen Electronic Organ, was completed in the spring of 1964.

Since its organization the following pastors have served our church:

Rev. J. Stadt	1877 - 1884
Rev. J. Gulker	1884 - 1890
Rev. E. Vanden Berg	1891 - 1893
Rev. E. Breen	1893 - 1903
Rev. I. Ven Deelen	1903 - 1907
Rev. J. Timmerman	1908 - 1916
Dr. R. L. Haan	1916 - 1924
Rev. N. J. Monsma	1924 - 1929
Dr. R. Bronkema	1929 - 1952
Rev. A Dusseljee	1952 - 1957
Rev. J. B. Hulst	1958 - 1965
Rev. R. H. Tjapkes	1966 - Present

For a small beginning with twelve families at its organization in 1871, the congregation today numbers 255 families, with a total number of 1136 individuals. Serving the congregation are the following organizations: A large and active Sunday School, Ladies Aid, "U Koninkrijk Kome", "Augustinus" Men's Society, Ladies "Faith, Hope and Love" Circle, Senior Christian Fellowship Society, Junior Christian Fellowship Society, Young People's Society, The Calvinettes, The Cadets, Ladies "Zangkoor", Mens' Psalm Singers, and a church choir. The congregation also enjoys the services of a fine library.

Presently serving the congregation is the Rev. R. H. Tjapkes. Our associate pastor is the Rev. A. L. Van Wyhe, Classical Home Missionary in Kansas City. Other missionaries are: Mr. Calvin Bruxvoort, Agana, Guam; Miss Ruth Haarsma, Jos, N. Nigeria; and Rev. Fred Diemer at Miami, Florida.

We thank and praise our faithful covenant God for his many manifestations of love and kindness and we hope and pray that He may continue to use us in the building of His church until the King of the church Himself shall return on the clouds of Heaven.

First Christian Reformed Church Consistory

Front row, left to right: Cornie Den Hartog, Nick Draayer, Randall Van Gelder, Marion De Vries, General Treasurer, Marion Jasper, John B. Reinders, Clerk; William Smit.

Second row, left to right: Peter Bylsma, Henry Haarsma, Vice President; Andrew Huisman, George Vande Kamp, Jr., Vernon Noteboom, Forrest Hubers, President of Deacons; Rev. Robert Tjapkes, President.

Back row, left to right: Dick Van Gelder, Secretary of Deacons; Tom I. De Jong, Otto Huizenga, Peter J. Jeltema, Merlyn Rowenhorst, Marion Andringa, Louis P. Wielenga.

Present building at Fourth St. and Arizona Ave. S.W.

American Reformed Church Consistory

Front row, left to right: Earl T. Klay, Clerk; Kenneth King, Forrest Van Oss, Rev. Alvin Hook, President; Lars Granberg, Frank W. Hulsart.

Back row, left to right: Paul Hudson, Roger Mouw, Don Vander Wel, Denis Rons, Gerard Kalsbeek, Robert Van Roekel, Carl Reinking, H. V. Rowenhorst, Wayne Reed, General Treasurer; Richard Deets, Building Fund Treasurer; Merlyn Kraai, Vice President (not shown).

The American Reformed Church

Rev. and Mrs. Alvin Hook

Present building at First St. and Arizona Ave. S.W.

The American Reformed Church in Orange City was organized as an English language church in the year 1885 for the benefit of those who could not understand the Dutch language. Twenty charter members comprised the congregation at the time of organization. The first edifice was erected in the year 1888, built upon a lot costing $100.00 at the corner of First and Arizona, where two succeeding buildings have been erected. The church will move to a new site on Albany Avenue where a larger edifice is nearing completion.

At the first congregational meeting held May 22, 1885, the Rev. J. A. De Spelder, the first principal of Northwestern Academy, was chosen to become the pastor. A few families came over from the First Reformed Church, but even so, the beginning was slow and difficult. This was due in some measure to what was called the misfortune of language superstition exhibited as soon as organization was completed.

The congregation lost two of its buildings by fire—the first one being struck by lightning in 1896, burning to the ground; the second one destroyed by fire on Friday evening, February 26, 1926.

Fourteen ministers have served the church dur-

ing the eighty-five years of its existence. The present pastor—the Rev. Alvin Hook—having served since 1958. The congregation at present supports eight missionaries in this country and abroad. Ten clergymen have come out of the congregation during the years and one young man is at present pursuing seminary training.

Approximately two hundred families comprise the membership, some four hundred and fifty members.

This church has drawn into its membership many people from various denominational backgrounds who have settled in Orange City. This makes the American Reformed Church an ecumenical-oriented congregation, characterized by breadth of vision and outgoing goodwill, yet solidly grounded in the fundamental revelation and teaching of the Gospel of Jesus Christ and the Reformed Protestant heritage.

The congregation is looking forward with great anticipation to the use of its new edifice—sancuary and educational unit—on Albany Avenue. The building committee hopes the congregation will be able to occupy the new facilities sometimes in in April or May with dedication services to be held shortly thereafter.

The Trinity Reformed Church

The Trinity Reformed Church was organized on July 15, 1919, as the third "Reformed" Church in Orange City. This organization came about as the result of fifteen families who left the First Reformed Church basically because of the desire and determination to use the English language in worship and education in the church for the benefit of their growing children. Permission to organize was granted by the Classis of West Sioux — the charter membership consisting of fifty-eight members in full communion and forty-seven baptized non-communicants. Trinity began and continued as a bi-lingual church until 1927 at which time she changed to the use of English only.

The Northwestern Academy Chapel served as the place of worship for the first four months, after this time the congregation moved to a temporary structure on the present church property. This structure, which stood where the present parsonage now stands, was called The Tabernacle. It was constructed by the men of the congregation in four days and dedicated on Thanksgiving Day of 1919. The congregation expanded rapidly and within a short time became crowded and hampered in work and worship by the lack of space. Consequently they began construction of a permanent church building in the spring of 1920. The cornerstone was laid June 11, 1920; the church was dedicated on March 18, 1921. This edifice, with the addition of a new education unit which was dedicated in September 1962, continues to serve as the center of worship for Trinity's three hundred seventy communicant members and one hundred eighty baptized non-communicants.

Beginning with the Charter Pastor, the Rev. John Steunenberg and continuing to the present, the congregation has been blessed with seven Undershepherds, each of whom in his own way has contributed to the nurture and growth of the church. Today, Trinity is vibrantly alive in her ministry, not only to her own families, but also to the community and world. This she has done by both sending out some twenty-three sons and daughters as ministers and missionaries as well as by rearing scores of sons and daughters who have and are taking their place in other areas of the world as witnesses for Christ.

Trinity Reformed Church and parsonage at Third Street and Albany Ave. N.E.

Consistory of the Trinity Reformed Church

Front Row — Left to Right   H. Dale Hubers; Clifford Bogaard, vice president; Rev. Donald Lenderink; A. J. Heemstra, clerk; Don E. Schreur, treasurer.

Back Row — Left to Right   Gordon McKinstrey; Paul Koets; Jacob L. Van Rooyen; Raymond Lubbers; Cliff Leslie; Paul Muyskens; Edward Lubbers; Paul Vander Kooi; William J. Berry; Roy Vander Stoep; Fred Kraai. (Willis Rozeboom, missing)

The history of Second Christian Reformed Church began almost fifty years ago. In the fall of 1920 a small group of families in the First Christian Reformed Church were concerned about the use of the Dutch language for the catechetical instruction of the youth. Their concern led them to petition their consistory for greater use of the English language. They were given permission to teach catechism in English, and classes were held for both the young and adults through the winter. In the spring the consistory of the Mother Church granted approval for English worship services. The group was permitted to use the chapel of Northwestern Classical Academy where morning and evening services were then conducted. Classis Orange City was petitioned for organization at its fall meeting and approval was granted. Five days later on September 26, 1921, the church was organized.

Prior to organization the congregation was able to construct its own building. Lots had been purchased from the Schalekamp Estate and with much donated labor, a tabernacle was built on the site. The tabernacle was meant to be a temporary structure but initial growth soon made it necessary that an extension of twenty-five feet be added to the building. In 1923, the congregation elected to build the present parsonage. The replacement of the tabernacle with a permanent house of worship did not occur until 1937. In that year the present church building was erected.

At the time of organization twenty-one families and eight individuals constituted the membership of the church. Altogether the congregation numbered 107 souls. This group chose as their first consistory A. Aardapple, W. W. Brower, and R. Cleveringa as elders; and J.A. Brink, J.R. Eerkes, and C.R. Mulder as deacons. Mr. Mulder also was

elected the first clerk. Charter members who still worship with us are Mrs. R. Cleveringa, Mr. and Mrs. J.S. De Groot, Mr. and Mrs. C.R. Mulder, Mr. F. Noteboom, Miss Anna Scholten and Mrs. Lou Wielinga.

From the beginning the Second Church was blessed with able ministers of the Word. The Reverend W.P. Van Wyk was the first to heed the call and served from 1922 to 1925. Other ministers and the years of their pastorate were: G. W. Hylkema 1925 - 1934, M.J. Vander Werp 1935 - 1940, A. Jabaay 1941 - 1944, R.O. De Groot 1945 - 1948, J. Masselink 1949 - 1958, H. Roelofs 1958 - 1965.

The present pastor, Jay De Vries took up the charge in 1966, Under his active leadership the church, now over 130 families, offers a program for all ages. Organizations include the Sunday School and Catechism through high school, the choir, Young Peoples Society, Couples Club, Mr. and Mrs. Club, Men's Society, the two Ladies Aids, Harmony Workers, and Benevolent Aid.

The congregation helps to maintain the mission program of the denomination and Christian education on all levels of learning. Above quota support is given to the missionary J. Pott and a native worker in Mexico, to missionary B. Nymer at Yakima, Washington and to mission churches in Salem, Oregon, and Kansas City, Kansas. Each year, young people participate in the S.W.I.M. program.

In recent years, the interior of the church has been extensively remodeled. The chancel was redone to accomodate a new pipe organ. New entrances, stairways and air conditioning were also installed.

The Lord has richly blessed Second Orange City during its first fifty years. May His house continue to be filled each Sunday with worshippers.

Dover Avenue Alliance Church

The Dover Avenue Alliance Church of Orange City had its beginnings in 1942 when a group of like-minded persons began to gather in homes for Bible study and prayer.

When the church was organized in 1944 it became known as The Orange City Gospel Church and the following people were charter members: Mrs. Elizabeth Bekman, Mr. and Mrs. Charles H. De Vries, Harvey G. De Vries, John Jacobs, Ruth Jacobs, Mr. and Mrs. Albert Kooy, Viola Kooy, Evageline Kooy, Mr. and Mrs. Joe Steensma, Mr. and Mrs. Andrew Vogel, Mr. and Mrs. Herman Wobbema, and Clarice Wobbema.

Rev. John H. Woodward, who had been conducting services in the homes, accepted the call to become the first pastor. The first annual business meeting and the first missionary convention took place in 1944. On January 11, 1945 a meeting was

called and, by unanimous decision, the present property located at 3rd and Dover Avenue N.E. was purchased. In March of 1945 services, which had been held in the Orange City Town Hall, were moved to the home on the newly purchased property. This home also served as the parsonage and is still in use as the parsonage today. During the year, the Middleburg Christian School building was purchased and moved to the property. After being remodeled for Worship and Sunday School facilities, the new church was dedicated in December of 1945.

Pastors who have faithfully served the church during its twenty-five years of existence include Rev. John Woodward, Rev. Harry Swanson, Rev. Richard Abrams, Rev. John Berentschot, Rev. Harley Heckman and Rev. David Hadley. The present pastor, Rev. Jacob Van Kekerix and his

Dover Avenue Alliance Church at Third St. and Dover Avenue N.E.

family arrived in Orange City in October of 1967 to take up his ministry among us.

For many years there was a strong desire to erect a new church which would more adequately serve the needs of a growing congregation. In September of 1965 the name of the church was changed to Dover Avenue Alliance Church and on October 31, 1965 the present edifice was consecrated with gratitude and thanksgiving.

From its inception the church has maintained a strong missionary interest, manifested through gifts and prayers. A number of young people have entered full-time Christian vocations. The church has maintained an affiliation with the Christian and Missionary Alliance, whose national headquarters are in New York and district headquarters in Omaha.

At the present time, regular services of the church include Sunday morning worship at 9:30 A.M., Sunday School classes for all ages at 10:45 A.M., Alliance Youth Fellowship at 6:30 P.M. and an evangelistic service at 7:30 P.M. Bible study and prayer, catechism classes, and choir rehearsal are held on Thursday evening. The Women's Missionary Society provides an opportunity for service to the local church as well as supplying the needs of home and foreign missionaries.

The 1969 board of the church is composed of the following members: Elders — Andrew Vogel John Jacobs, David Crockett, Cornelius Pals; Deacons — Marvin Vogel, Harold Pals, and Albert Mouw.

The desire of the congregation of the Dover Avenue Alliance Church is that we might be of service to those in our community and that we might do our part to faithfully proclaim the Gospel of Jesus Christ at home and to the far corners of the earth.

Dover Avenue Alliance Executive Committee

Front Row – Left to Right   Arthur Vogel, treasurer; John Jacobs, vice president of the elders; Peter Van Vugt; Cornelius Pals

Back Row – Left to Right   Marvin Vogel, Sunday School superintendent; Rev. J. Van Kekerix, president; Roger Roghair, secretary; Harold Pals, vice president of the deacons.

Rev. and Mrs. A. E. Kleppinger

Assembly Of God Church

On June 1, 1958, the Home Missions Department of the Iowa District of the Assemblies of God, with Headquarters in Des Moines, chose Rev. and Mrs. A.E. Kleppinger to pioneer the church in Orange City, Iowa. The Assemblies of God purchased a church and parsonage on Third and Delaware South West in Orange City, Iowa, from the Protestant Reformed group. During their first year in Orange City, the pastor and other friends remodeled the church and parsonage, also making general repairs. The work has progressed slowly but surely. There have always been worshippers since the church was opened.

The five Cardinal doctrines of the Assemblies of God are:
Salvation through faith in the atoning blood of Christ;
Divine Healing in answer to the prayer of faith; the Baptism of the Holy Ghost;
the Bible evidence of speaking in other tongues as the Spirit gives utterance;
and the imminent Return of Christ to take away all saints dead and alive who love and look for His coming from heaven.

The Assemblies of God has been a leader in the Pentecostal Movement which began around 1900. It was established as a denomination in 1914. It was organized to bring a renewal of the Holy Spirit as in the early (Bible Days) church period. This Charismatic Renewal is now spreading to the old line historic churches. The Assemblies of God now has over 1900 foreign Missionaries, 10,000 ministers and 8,500 churches.

Pastor Kleppinger and his church feel a genuine call to Orange City to share their experiences with all people inside and outside the churches.

Assembly of God church at Third St. and Delaware Ave. S. W.

Orange City – Alton Lutheran Mission

The beginnings of the Orange City – Alton Lutheran Church must actually be traced to the hard work and foresight of all the people living in Orange City and Alton. For as your community grew, due to your labors to build a pleasant community, others were drawn to your midst by the fruits of your labors. Among those were your Lutheran neighbors. As time passed your Lutheran neighbors grew in number and so did their desire to worship in their own Lutheran church. Your community atmosphere of good will and willingness to help came to the aid of your Lutheran neighbors.

Of course, no church is ever established without the tireless, faithful efforts of its people. In this instance countless conversations between Lutherans led to a group meeting in April 1969 of Lutherans living in the Orange City - Alton area. Subsequent meetings and discussions led to the choice of The Lutheran Church-Missouri Synod as the major Lutheran body that the new mission would be affiliated with. Many of you probably better know this synod as "The Church of The Lutheran Hour" or by its connection with the television production "This Is The Life." On November 19, 1969 interested Lutherans in the area elected a Steering Committee of seven to carry on the work of organization. The Rev. John F. Hargreaves, pastor of Peace Lutheran Church, Marcus, was to serve the new mission, and Peace, Marcus also agreed to "mother" the new mission. Northwestern College offered the use of its chapel on January 11, 1970. Future plans call for the purchase of land and the erection of worship and educational facilities that will be a credit to the community.

Local Pastors

Front Row – Left to Right Rev. Donald Lenderink; Rev. A. E. Kleppinger; Rev. A. Hook; and Rev. Robert H. Tjapkes
Back Row – Left to Right Rev. Jay De Vries; Rev. Alvin J. Eissens; Rev. Jacob Van Kekerix; and Dr. R. Van Heukelom

CONCLUSION

Orange City is not a microcosm of the American church world. It is largely Protestant, and Biblical in the orthodox sense; and the church membership of the community is close to 100% of the population. Its churches, conscious of the Biblical mandates to "Teach Jesus Christ and Him crucified" and to claim the world for Jesus Christ, are proud and grateful for their Christian heritage. They trust and hope and pray that the King of the Church will continue to bless th em as He has in the past to the end that His Name may be honored and praised, on earth even as in Heaven.   *Soli Deo Gloria!*

The Lafayette School had been in Orange City almost from the start, since education was a necessity in the eyes of the first settlers. Crowded schools are a common complaint today, but at least some teachers, buildings, and equipment are available. The pioneers had to provide everything from scratch. Grasshopper years compounded the difficulties, and overcrowding could not be avoided. When May Noteboom started school in 1888, pupils had to sit three abreast in double seats. Then as now "kids" were mischievous, and often the smaller ones were pushed off the seats into the aisle. But the fundamentals, reading, writing, and arithmetic, were hammered home. Penmanship must have been stressed, since the writing of those days usually was beautifully spaced and uniformly slanted.

School Days

Public School 1895—Back row: Mr. L. Scholten, Janitor; Josephine De Booy (Mrs. Franken), Miss Reece, Mr. J. C. Trainer, Mr. O. W. Kerr, Sarah Hospers (Mrs. P. D. Van Oosterhout), Lulu Robinson (Mrs. Christian). Middle row: Gerrit Muilenburg (son of Teunis), Kathryn Vos (Mrs. W. W. Schultz), Sue Johnson. Front row: Prof. Philip Soulen, Music Teacher; Mr. G. W. Gross, Superintendent, Lillian Hutchinson, Nora Held (Mrs. Hubert Rynsberger).

A Country School of 1884-1886

The attendance record book of one school southwest of Orange City was in a box of books sold to Ray De Jong when the school and contents were sold. The "Daily Program of Recitation and Study" included Bible, reading, arithmetic, writing, geography, history, spelling, grammer, and physiology. Later, mental arithmetic, drawing, and composition were added. Pupils were classed according to the "Reader" they were able to master. Older children, who went to school only in the winter, were obliged to sit in with younger pupils. In fall and spring these older pupils had to help with the home and farm work and were kept out of school. Some of the teachers, who often boarded at the homes of the students, are mentioned in the record book:

Thos. B. David—March 31, 1884 - July 17, 1884
George R. Moir—November 17, 1884 - March 6, 1885
Ella Mann—March 30, 1885 - June 19, 1885
Agnes Moir—Spring term of 1886
Frank Spinden—Winter term of 1886-1887
J. F. Vanden Berg—1887
Kate Peuse—March 25, 1889 - July 11, 1891
H. Rhynsburger—Winter term. He later taught in the town school.

Others were R. Maxwell, Ira M. Jackson, Kate Purse, Carrie Wicks, H. H. Spinden, and Addie Brown.

The names of many of the following pupils are familiar. The babies of the pioneers, they are the parents and grandparents of many present Orange City residents.

Minnie Van Peursem	10	Dennis Hollander	7
Martin Van Peursem	6	Roelof Cleveringa	6
Albert Brink	8	Abe Cleveringa	5
Henry Brink	8	John De Jong	12
William Van Peursem	12	Katie De Jong	5
Peter De Jong	10	Henry De Jong	6
Jeanette De Jong	8	Hattie De Jong	6
Minnie De Jong	7	Arie De Boer	5
Emma De Boer	8	John Van Peursem	7
Sallie Hollander	9	Minnie J. De Jong	7
Antonna Kots	13	Minnie Brink	5
Peter Van Roekel	6	John Van Roekel	8
Willie Labberton	7		

New Pupils enrolled during the next year 1884-1885:

Albert Younred		Fannie De Roos	5
John Van Peursem	8	Susie Cambier	12
Henry Van Peursem	14	Nellie Cambier	7
Peter Van Peursem	16	Peter Cambier	7
Conrad De Jong	5	Jennie Cambier	5
Conrad De Jong	16	Grace Van Roekel	6
Peter Van Wyk	16	Willie Brink	5
Garret Van Peursem	5	Garret Labberton	5
Thomas Hollander	8	Lena Ter Horst	12
Arie De Boer	6	Minnie Brink	6
Sippie Rederbur	6	Garret Brink	5
Anna De Roos	11		

The school building at Maurice

Junior High School building

Most of the pioneer children did not have the opportunity for higher education. Those who had great desire became self-educated, and their influence was felt in religious, political, and business positions. The shortage of teachers was less acute and changes less frequent when the graduates of Northwestern Academy and nearby high schools began to teach. They often boarded with patron parents and walked or drove buggies to school.

Two sisters were widely respected for their teaching abilities. Miss Sue De Lint taught for thirteen years in a school in Holland Township, and her sister Tena served in a school southwest of Orange City for eleven years. They also taught in other schools, including the Orange City system. Their sister Ann still lives in Orange City.

Then as now, pupils and teachers did have their troubles. One day a principal was supervising the study period in the absence of Mr. Rhynsberger, the regular teacher. He suggested to the pupils that he need not say anything about whispering. At the end of the period he asked who had whispered. Every hand went up and all were kept after school. Some had to walk two miles and did not get home until late. Mary Noteboom's mother became worried. Since she had not seen the neighbor Fred Nieuwendorp pass by either, she feared something might have gone wrong and became quite upset. Little Mary is now eighty-seven years old, and she vows that was the only time she was ever kept after school, and then only because John De Bey whispered to her first.

Orange City Public School

It might be said that the first public school in Orange City was in a house. During the fall and winter of 1870 — 1871, Mr. John Van De Steeg taught school in the home of his father, Gerrit Van De Steeg. During August, 1871, the first school building was completed with the school year beginning in September of that year. In November of 1872 there were a total of sixty-six pupils in the Orange City Public School.

In March of 1948, a fire of unknown origin destroyed the old grade school building. A contract was awarded in July of 1948 for the construction of a new building to replace that destroyed by fire.

On Monday, June 9, 1958, an election was held on re-organization of several independent districts into one district to be known as Maurice-Orange City Community School District. The areas included in the election were all or parts of the following: Holland Township, Maurice Independent School District, Nassau Township, Orange City Independent District, Reading Township, Sherman Township, West Branch Township. The final meeting of the Board of Directors of the Orange City Independent School District was held on June 30, 1958. The first meeting of the Board of Directors of the Maurice-Orange City Community School was held on July 1, 1958. Members of the Board included Wayland Breese, Martin Raak, E. B. Grossman, Howard Ruisch, and Elmer Van Roekel.

On January 10, 1967 the District passed a $1,141,660,000 bond proposal providing for a new high school building and an addition to the Junior High School building in Maurice. The new high school is located on East Highway No. 10. Members of the Board of Education at the time work was begun on the new high school were: R. J. Hassebroek, Martin Raak, Lorenz Mouw, Wallace Muilenburg, Duane Van Der Weide.

The new high school was completed in July 1969 with the first classes being held in August 1969.

From the first public school enrollment of sixty-six pupils during the 1871 - 1872 school year, the fall of 1969 total enrollment was 865.

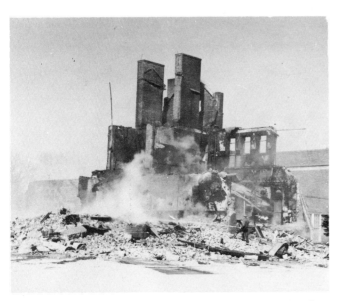

Taken after the fire at the Orange City Public School on the night of March 13, 1948.

Maurice-Orange City Board of Education
Standing—Left to right: Lorenz Mouw, Wallace Muilenburg, Vice President; Duane Vande Weide, Marty Raak.
Seated—Left to right: Lorraine Alberts, Secretary; R. J. Hassebroek, President; Frank Hulst, Superintendent.

The New Maurice-Orange City High School opened for the 1969-70 school year.

Foot Ball Team of 1933 Orange City High School

Left to right — Back Row: Gerald Kraai, Merlyn Kraai, Hubert Noteboom, Russell Kraai, Alvin Houtsma, John Cambier, Don Van Peursem, Coach Mark McLarnan. Front Row: Robert Dunlop, Gilbert Giebink, Vernon Van De Schoor, Benjamin Ver Steeg, Robert Fisher, Victor Bekman, Robert Giebink.

Basket Ball Team of 1930 Orange City High School

Left to Right — Back Row: Coach Karges, Melvin Synhorst, Wilbur Ver Steeg, Russell Kraai, Gilbert Giebink, William Duistermars, Vernon De Haan, Supt. Mr. R. C. Ross. Front row: Charles Tye, Paul Klein, Leonard Melles, Raymond Kraai, Wesely Pass.

Basket Ball Team of 1934 - 35 Orange City High School

Left to right — Front Row: Coach Frank L. Kinch, Lloyd De Jong, Robert Dunlop, Merlyn Kraai, Irwin Muilenberg, Don Dunlop. Back Row: Perry Dingman, Jack Van Wyk, Gerald Kraai, Ray Van Pelt, Earl Klay, Carl Van De Waa

Maurice-Orange City High School "Pride of the Dutchmen" Band

Orange City Christian School

1904

First Orange City Christian School
At right of picture: Principal Mr. Benjamin Masselink; teachers: Miss Dena Van Der Burg and Miss Kitty De Kraay. Janitor: Mr. Slickers.

90

The eight room school building built in 1918

The movement to organize a Society for Christian Instruction in Orange City began in 1903. Much of the impetus toward such a society was provided by the leadership of Rev. I. Van Dellen. The society was formally organized on September 7, 1903.

Those serving on the first school board included T. H. Smidt, H. De Vries, H. Mulder, J. Wiersma, A. Cupido, P. Mouw, W. Vellinga, O. J. Bijlsma, and G. Kroeze.

The board purchased the vacant two-room Ward School and moved it to property also purchased at that time on Pella Street (now Colorado Avenue between 3rd and 4th Streets).

On September 5, 1904 classes were begun with a very serious dilemma — the building was too small for the 100 pupils who enrolled! While classes were held elsewhere, a second story was added to the building that first year.

December 19, 1907 stands out in memory. The school basement had been piled full of old dry shingles for fuel. Someone entered the building that night and set fire to these shingles. Though a sizeable amount of shingles burned, as the school's 50th anniversary states it, "God had put the fire out!"

In February, 1918 the school society decided to build a new eight room school. It was also during that year that the school suffered along with the community as a result of the influenza epidemic.

In 1920 the school became a charter member of the National Union of Christian Schools and has taken an active part in this organization throughout ensuing years.

Because the school's financial support comes primarily from tuition and gifts, great difficulty was experienced during the depression years. In 1932, for instance, all teachers agreed to a cancellation of set wages and expressed a willingness to work for whatever support might come in. Much time and labor was donated to provide wood for furnace fuel.

Throughout the following years the school continued steady growth in enrollment, financial support, and curriculum. On February 25, 1954 the society decided to purchase the present school property and build a new building. This was dedicated in 1956. In 1962 the east or junior high classroom wing was completed and dedicated so that presently the school contains 13 classrooms, a music room, a centralized library and a multi-purpose room. A full curriculum is offered, including art, music, band, and remedial reading, with a staff of fourteen full-time and six part-time faculty members.

Indeed, those supporting the school have had ample reasons throughout the years to exclaim the truth of Numbers 23:23, "What hath God wrought!" Soli Deo Gloria!

Orange City Christian School

Monica Society

The Monica Society of the Orange City Christian School was organized in 1921 with the purpose of serving various Christian institutions with financial and moral support.

However, in 1929, it was decided to work solely for the Christian School. The Dutch language was used until 1934. The name of the society was chosen by Mr. and Mrs. C. Aue, because "Monica" was the faithful and praying mother of her wayward son St. Augustine. The first meetings were held in the homes of members where many hours were spent making rugs, blankets, and the like for their annual sale which is still held every year.

One of the highlights of the year is an all-day picnic which is held in either the Reinsma grove, Ter Horst grove, or a nice spot along the Floyd River.

The society is also noted for its dialogues, humorous Yankee Dutch readings, and renditions on the musical saws.

We now have a third generation working for the school with sixty-three active and one hundred fifty associate members. Some of the present day projects are food stands at Tulip Time and the Ball Park, soup suppers, bake sales, catering, and our annual sale of handwork.

From the years 1934 to 1970 the society has given approximately $90,000 to the school. Records for the twelve previous years are not available.

Unity Christian High School Faculty

Standing, left to right: Dennis Pluimer, Andrew Miedema, Gary Regnerus, Carl Vander Muelen, Ken Vos, Ronald Zwiers, Phares Lefever.

Seated, left to right: Mrs. David Hensley, Mrs. Peter Pals, Howard Hall, Administrator, Mrs. Ken Vos.

Unity Christian High School

For many years the idea of a Christian Secondary School in Orange City lay dormant in the minds of several people. The idea was given impetus a few years ago by a Western Christian High Long Range Planning Committee which suggested a possibility of establishment of another school to answer the problem of facilities.

An organizational meeting was held November 27, 1962. Mr. George Vogel presided at this historic meeting and a society was formed to study the feasibility of opening a new Christian High School in Orange City. A second meeting was held February 4, 1963, and the name Unity Christian High School Association was adopted. A decision was made to instruct the Board of Trustees to purchase a site and proceed with the development of plans with a goal in mind of opening the school in September of 1964.

On September 5, 1963, the third meeting of the society was held. The constitution and by-laws were adopted. Building plans were also approved by the society. The fourth meeting was held September 4, 1964. The first budget was approved and a report was received by the first administrator Dr. Werkema.

The original Board of Trustees was composed of nine members. They were: Tom I. De Jong, George Vogel, Andy Van Dyk, Ralph Bouma, Rev. Harlan Roelofs, Jerald Dykstra, Percy Bylsma, Lee Woudstra, and Chester Van Peursem. This group signed the articles of incorporation which was instituted February 4, 1963. The purpose of the corporation was stated: "The object and purpose of this corporation shall be to establish, conduct and maintain a school or schools for Christian education for instruction and to promote God's glory in all matters which concern Christian secondary education." On August 28, 1964, seventy-seven students enrolled in Unity Christian High for the ninth and tenth grade. Grades eleven and twelve were added in 1965 and 1966. The first graduating class received their diplomas on May 23, 1967.

During the year 1968, another building project took place. The Association instructed the Board of Trustees to begin building a physical education and music addition. This was completed in October of 1968 and a full physical education program was instituted.

Today there are 222 students enrolled at Unity Christian High with a senior class of forty-nine members, there are fifty-nine students in the junior class, forty-nine in the sophomore class and sixty-five in the freshman class.

At the present time there are eleven full-time faculty members and two part-time instructors:

Principal—Howard Hall
Bible — Anne De Vries
Business—Typing — Conrad Harthoorn
German — Phares Lefever
American History — Guidance Counselor — Andy Miedema
Science — Dennis Pluimer
Social Studies — Gary Regnerus
Physical Education — Rick Vander Berg
English — Carl Vandermeulen
English — Grace Vos
Physics — Math — Ken Vos
Music — Ronald Zwiers
Part-time Music — Nancy Hensley
Part-time Librarian — Helen Pals

The present Board of Trustees members are:
President - Forrest Hubers
Secretary — Gilbert Byker
Treasurer — Ralph Bouma
Vice President — Russell Maatman
General Adjutant — Peter I. Noteboom
Other Board Members — Ken Huisman, Stewart Goslinga, John Broek, and Junior Dooyema.

The Unity emblem was designed by a committee of the 1964 - 1965 Student Council. It was adopted by the Board of Trustees to be the official emblem of the school. The design emphasizes three significant facts: the fact that the cross of Jesus Christ dominates our lives, the fact that the Holy Scriptures presents to us the truth of God, and the fact that the cross of Jesus Christ and the Holy Scriptures provide a shield for us to protect us against those who would destroy the truth of Scripture and the cross. The emblem is used whenever a symbolic representation of the school's foundation is needed.

Unity Christian High School Finance Board — Front row, left to right: John Obbink, Secretary; Elmer Duistermars, Vice President; Clarence Postma, President; Gary Kroeze, Recording Treasurer. Back row, left to right: Harvey Pluim, Arthur Kalsbeek, John Droog, Peter Mars.

Unity Christian High School Board of Trustees — Front row, left to right: Gilbert Byker, Secretary; Ralph Bouma, Treasurer; Forrest Hubers, President; Dr. Russell Maatman, Vice President. Back row, left to right: Peter Noteboom, General Assistant; John Broek; Howard Hall, Administrator; Junior Dooyema, Stewart Goslinga, Ken Huisman.

The College

Pioneers are extraordinary people. Faced with the uncertainties of survival in a new land they never-the-less have the audacity to dream dreams. Thus it was with the Dutch families who moved from Pella to Sioux County in 1870.

They dreamed dreams for their new colony. One dream was the establishment of an institution of higher learning based on Christian principles. Despite persistent grasshopper plagues and the inevitable economic hardships that go with opening a new land Northwestern Classical Academy was founded in 1882.

The Academy was founded to "provide a good education premised on the Christian faith as interpreted by Reformed theology." An immediate goal was to train youth for the ministry and teaching. Within a short time the Academy was receiving support from the area congregations as well as from the local faithful. Its teaching ministry began in September, 1883, in the consistory room of the First Reformed Church of Orange City with three grades and three part-time teachers and two dozen pupils. In early 1884 classes were moved to a temporary classroom on the present site of the college, and "The Pioneer School" was a reality. From 1886 to 1895, the Academy functioned in an abandoned skating rink from which it moved to Zwemer Hall. During the same period the school's enrollment grew from 25 to some 74; and its teaching staff from one principal-teacher, the Rev. John De Spelder, in 1884 to four full-time teachers in 1902.

To implement its purpose of long term rather than immediate relevance, Northwestern Academy sought to "lay a thorough foundation of liberal education"; thus, though other courses of study were added, the classical nature of its studies long persisted. By 1903 the school was on the accredited list of Iowa colleges; and in March, 1930, it was formally accepted into the North Central Accrediting Association. A large proportion of the school's graduates became teachers, ministers, doctors, lawyers, and businessmen; this was especially true of the early graduates, a testimony to the quality of education given from the very beginning.

There was early talk of a college; the Sioux County Herald, the American newspaper, spoke of such "aspirations" at the time of the Academy's founding. Approved by the Board of Trustees in June, 1926, the junior college division began classes in September of 1928 with an enrollment of 30 students. The junior college department grew steadily, gradually eclipsing the Academy and modifying the Academy's curriculum until it was similar to that of most high schools.

In May, 1949, the General Synod of the Reformed Church removed the two-year limitation on Northwestern, making it possible for the insti-

Ramaker Library

tution to meet the requirements for a four-year teacher training program. In 1965 the Board of Trustees endorsed a broader liberal arts program, in order to provide a thorough Christian education in the Reformed tradition through the means of a liberal arts education.

Accreditation and Association

The Junior College received accreditation by the North Central Association in 1953; the full college received preliminary accreditation as a four-year college in June, 1964. Its degree program received the approval of the Iowa Department of Public Instruction. Northwestern is a member of the Association of American Colleges, the American Association of University Women, the National Commission of Accrediting, the Association of American Colleges for Teacher Education, the Iowa Association of Private Colleges and Universities, the Iowa College Foundation, and the Colleges of Mid-America, a consortium of eleven church sponsored colleges located in northwest Iowa and eastern South Dakota.

The Campus

Prominent on its sixty-five acre campus is Ramaker Library. The library presently houses more than 50,000 volumes; a Dutch Heritage Room with books and documents of historic interest plus the complete files of "De Volksvriend", a former Orange City Dutch newspaper; numerous periodicals and other reference materials. The papers and books of former Congressman Charles B. Hoeven, who represented Northwest Iowa for 22 years in the United States Congress, has been given a special place in the library. In February, 1970, Ramaker Library was declared a selective depository for United States government documents. The only other such depository in the area is in the Sioux City Public Library.

Other recent additions to the campus include a Mathematics-Science-Foreign Language classroom building, a Student Union-Women's Dormitory and the Women's Dormitory and campus dining hall located on the south campus. Central to the

College South Dormitory Built in 1969

Dr. Lars Granberg

Student Union at Northwestern College

campus is Zwemer Hall, a constant reminder of the heritage from the past.

From a Junior College with thirty students and a faculty of ten, who also taught in the Academy Department, the institution enrolled a student body of 153 in 1953 with a faculty of 19 for both departments at the time of its accreditation by the North Central Association. In 1957, when the four year Teacher Education Program was begun, the college had 215 students with a full-time faculty of 19. Since the Academy's existence was terminated in June, 1961, the college has grown to an enrollment of over 700 students and a faculty which now numbers 52 full-time and 3 part-time.

Numerous individuals played important roles in Northwestern's history. Henry Hospers donated the main campus site. The Rev. Seine Bolks, first pastor of the First Reformed Church, was the first president of the Academy's Board of Trustees. Some of the great teachers of the early years included Henry Pietenpol, Thomas Welmers, Mae Brugge, and A. J. Muste. The Rev. Dr. Jacob

Heemstra served as president from 1928 to 1951. Dr. Heemstra guided the school through the difficult depression days. Contemporaries of Dr. Heemstra who contributed invaluable services to Northwestern were Attorney Anthony Te Paske of Sioux Center, Elder Henry De Groot of Orange City, and the Rev. Henry Colenbrander, pastor of the First Reformed Church, Orange City.

Dr. Frederick Wezeman followed Dr. Heemstra in the presidency and led the college during the years of Junior College certification.

Dr. Preston Stegenga's effective years were marked by rapid growth. His administration reshaped Northwestern into a four-year teachers' college. Under Dr. Stegenga's leadership many of the buildings which make up the present campus were completed, and the four-year teacher education program received accreditation.

Dr. Lars Granberg, current president, has been charged by the college trustees with the task of guiding the college into a quality four-year Christian liberal arts college. Good progress is being made toward this goal.

Ramaker Library at Northwestern College

The Alumni Garden, a gift of the alumni

The Bushmer Art Center, a gift of Dr. and Mrs. A. Bushmer 1968

Northwestern College Auxiliary Officers

Left to right: Mrs. Ray Wierda, Alton, Iowa, Secretary; Mrs. Alfred Aalberts, Orange City, President; Mrs. Virgil Rowenhorst, Orange City, Treasurer; Mrs. S. Scorza, Orange City, Vice President.

Women's Auxiliary of Northwestern College

Realizing that the success of a school depends on efficient leadership and active cooperation of the people it serves, an Auxiliary of Northwestern College and Academy was organized in 1928, by a group of women interested in promoting the welfare of the school. The officers, with Mrs. Rev. Jacob Heemstra as president, had a great deal of faith in their undertaking. By combining their talents with much hard work this new organization boasted of 300 members within a year. Immediately they began appropriating substantial funds to meet the extreme needs of the school. To raise the money they collected yearly dues from their members and served meals for the school's banquets and faculty dinners. Through the years they have served many banquets for city and community organizations including the Lion's Club, the Women's Club, the R E C, Girl's Leagues, N. Club, etc. Other fund raising projects have included Silver Teas, the sale of cook books, eating stands in the park at Tulip Time, the sale of aprons at Tulip Time, Harvest Festival Auctions, and Song Fests. Hundreds of letters are sent out yearly to members, alumni, and guilds of the denomination seeking cash donations to our "Little Apron" fund. Cakes are baked and sold for birthday celebrations of dormitory students.

Some of the smaller but much needed items given to the school included a piano, a memeograph machine, choir gowns, a library charging desk, a Christian Flag, a furnace, shrubs and trees, and a public address system. During the lean years, the Auxiliary gave thousands of dollars to the college for operating expenses. Undertaking these projects stimulated the best efforts of everyone.

In recent years the larger gifts included:

$26,650 to Ramaker Library
   4,485 for redecorating of classrooms, dormitories, lounges, and improvements in the President's Home.
 15,000 for the building of the President's Home
 33,625 equipping 3 kitchens and furnishings for 2 dormitories

To date our gifts to the college total well over $100,000.

All these gifts have been of great assistance to Northwestern. However, the contributions have not all been material. The Auxiliary has helped to create a deeper interest in Christian Education among the women of the church. It has stimulated an appreciation in Northwestern throughout the entire community and in ever widening areas.

Northwestern College Central Mall

Dawn Swet—1970 Tulip Festival Queen

Tulip Time

Vivid memories of recent Tulip Festivals linger in the minds of all local citizens — the months of planning, preparation and hard work culminating in a springtime burst of color, music, and pageantry. But the distant past is not as easily recalled, and records of events leading up to Orange City's first Tulip Festival are rather meager and indefinite. The Hollanders' innate tendency toward cleanliness and beauty combined with a historical background of flower culture is an acceptable, although abstract motivating force. This force found physical expression as early as 1935, when it was recorded that in addition to the large number of tulip plantings already in existence in Orange City, some 50,000 more bulbs were imported and planted by the townspeople. Combining the tulip planting project with the organized efforts of the Orange City Chamber of Commerce, in 1936 the ground work was laid for the beginning of the now nationally-publicized Tulip Festival.

Accounts of activities in the April and May issues of the 1936 Sioux County Capital indicate that the first festival, May 14, featured a parade, costume contest, LeMars Drum and Bugle Corps, Better Homes and Gardens photographer's staff, The Friesian Society Sing, window displays of Holland momentos, American Legion concessions,

Northwestern Junior College Chorus and Orange City High School Band, and in the evening a concert by the Sioux City Symphony Orchestra.

The outstanding innovation of the 1937 festival was the election and coronation of the first Tulip Queen, Elizabeth Top (Swets). The next year an elaborate and formal coronation ceremony was introduced into the program, involving not only the Queen and her attendants, but a score or more of additional personnel as guards, ushers, trumpeters, etc. Ceremonial functions have, throughout the twenty-five years, been carried out by City Officials and Iowa's Vice Council for the Netherlands, also a local citizen. With minor changes this ceremony is still considered one of the most colorful and impressive attractions of the festival.

Because of the public interest in the Tulip Festival and the consequential large crowds attending, 1938 marked the first year of two-day festivities. The entire program of activities was repeated each day and on each evening. "In Dutch", a musical comedy in two acts, locally composed and cast, was staged at the City Auditorium.

During the next three years — 1939, 1940, and 1941 — the general trend of festivities followed the established pattern, and interest in the festival grew in unexpected proportions. Each year thous-

Street Scrubbers in action.

107

Waterboys with yokes and buckets do the heavy work for the street scrubbers.

ands of additional tulip bulbs were imported, and substantial gifts of bulbs were received from the Netherlands Bulb Growers Association.

The war years followed, and from 1942 through 1946 festivities were replaced by Victory Days and other appropriate observance events. In the fall of 1946 50,000 new bulbs were imported and planted in anticipation of the 1947 festival. The Dutch Street Dancers, performing Dutch Folk Dances in full Dutch regalia, including wooden shoes, made their debut in 1947. Their rhythmic and precision performance has since been one of the big attractions of the Festival.

During the next three years the renewed interest and enthusiasm was so widespread that in 1950 the Tulip Festival Steering Committee found it both necessary and desirable to institute a three-day festival. Requests representing thousands of interested folks from cities such as Sioux Falls and Sioux City, unable to attend except on Saturdays, and from schools on behalf of teachers and pupils alike, were strong inducements for the now established three-day festival including a Saturday.

1950 was one of the climactic years because of the attendance, as special guest, of His Excellency E. N. Van Kleffen, Netherlands Ambassador to the United States. This momentous event, in addition to the three-day festival, made total attendance soar to new heights. The evening show marked the revival of a home talent production "Tulip Time Musical" which included the operetta "Tulip Time in Holland".

The musical program which was given at the Tulip Festival in 1938. Name of the play "In Dutch". Book, Lyrics and Music by Mr. A. J. Kolyn Orchestration of score by Mrs. Earl Gary. A few of the songs were "Every Day is Ladies' Day with Me" and "You Can't Beat the Dutch".

The year 1951 marked the beginning of a new era in home talent production of the evening show. Victor Herbert's "The Red Mill" was a complete sell-out, with hundreds of admission requests turned down, "The Red Mill" was repeated in 1952 with even more enthusiastic response. In 1953 the committee felt that a change might be acceptable, and Victor Herbert's "Sweethearts" was presented to overflow crowds for four evenings. In 1954 and 1955 these two productions were presented alternately with local color innovations and with continued enthsiastic reception by the public.

In 1956 the committee in charge felt that the home talent personnel had earned a season of relaxation, and succeeded in booking the nationally famous Male Quartet known to Radio and Television as "The Mariners."

The next six years were highlighted by the advent of a professional wooden shoemaker from The Netherlands; the Premier showing of "The Willow Man," and a completely new method of selecting the Tulip Queen by a panel of judges assisted by the public.

Group of Dutch Street Dancers performing on Sioux City streets as part of Booster Trip caravan.

Throughout the years after the Second World War the general program has followed a definite pattern, briefly summarized in the following outline:

Each morning —
    Dutch Antique Museum at City Auditorium
    Tulip Exhibits — all tulip gardens open to to visitors.

1:30 P.M. — Dutch Street Program
    Street Inspection
    Street Scrubbing
    Parade of decorative floats and marching bands.
    Festival Queen's Coronation
    Street Dancers — 250 girls in costume and Klompen

7:00 P.M.
    Parade of floats and marching bands
    Dutch Street Dancers

8:15 P.M.
    Local talent production, City Auditorium
    Presentation of Tulip Queen and Attendants

Festivals of the 1960 decade have hosted many guests of national fame from educational, social, and political categories. Internationally the festival has drawn attention, most recently by the visit of two of our queens as festival Ambassadors to The Netherlands.

Evening entertainment has featured such stage hit productions as "Carousel," "South Pacific," "Sound of Music," "The Music Man," and "Oliver".

One of the special events of the decade occurred in 1965 when all former queens were invited to attend and receive special recognition and honors. Nostalgic atmosphere was enhanced by again staging Victor Herbert's "The Red Mill" as the night entertainment.

Although the general program has followed a definite pattern, those who serve on the many committees are particularly aware of the myraids of changes, additions, and refinements appearing each year. These unnoticed developments produce the "overtones" which keep this annual festival ever new.

Authentic Dutch Street Organ. Obtained from The Netherlands during Netherlands' Trade Fair in Philadelphia 1950.

Mr. Jensen carving out wooden shoes for The Mariners while they wait.

On April 8, 1954 the Booster Club of Trinity Reformed Church decided on a project for Community benefit. The Pastor Charles Boonstra commenced correspondence with sources in the Netherlands with the hope of arranging for some one skilled in the art of making Wooden Shoes to emigrate to Orange City.

His efforts bore fruit when two years later August 16, 1956, Mr. and Mrs. Willem Jansen and two children arrived to become residents of Orange City, and later gaining Citizenship in the United States.

Through community cooperative Mr. Jansen set up shop for the manufacture of wooden shoes.

As far as can be determined he is the only manufacturer of wooden shoes west of the Mississippi River. Today his unique product is shipped into almost every State.

The Jansen family and his wooden shoes have added much to the colorful Dutch Heritage of Orange City.

Klompen–"Wooden Shoes"

The factory where the Jensen family worked since coming from the Netherlands.

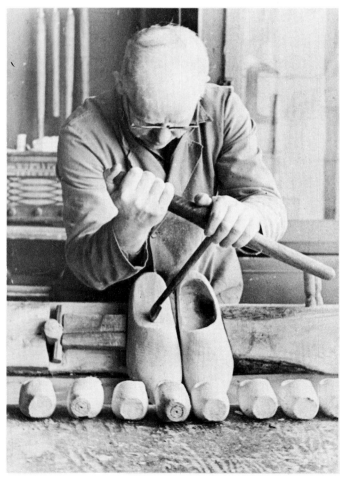

Mr. Jensen putting the finishing touches on a pair of shoes.

113

Gerrit Klay, Iowa's Vice Council to The Netherlands, crowning Katherine Lubbers Royal Queen—1938

Front row, left to right: Marvella Huisman Duistermars, Rita Van Steenwyk Van Oort, Betty Mulder Reinders, Helen Beyer Hull, Bertha Visser Van Gelder, Ann Schoep Groen, Elizabeth Top Swets, Karen Mouw De Haan.

Back row, left to right: Judy Raak, Jean Miller Anderson, Linda Van Klompenberg Massman, Karen Bogaard Keithley, Mary Lou Korver Vander Wel, Audrey Korver Scholten, Carol Bomgaars Groeneweg, Shirlee Vogelaar Arenson.

Tulip Queens Through The Years

1937	Elizabeth Top Swets		1956	Shirlee Vogelaar Arneson
1938	Katherine Lubbers Royal		1957	Carol Bomgaars Groeneweg
1939	Anna Schoep Groen		1958	Frieda Brower Scharf
1940	Bertha Visser Van Gelder		1959	Audrey Korver Scholten
1941	Marjorie Brower Van Lummel		1960	Mary Lou Korver Vander Wel
1942 - 46	World War II		1961	Karen Bogaard Keithley
1947	Darlene Vande Berge Kiernan		1962	Linda Van Klompenburg Massman
1948	Helen Beyer Hull		1963	Jean Miller Anderson
1949	Betty Mulder Reinders		1964	Judy Raak
1950	Rita Van Steenwyk Van Oort		1965	Barbara Jacobs Lubbers
1951	Marvella Huisman Duistermars		1966	Pamela Mulder Nelson
1952	Joyce Wiersma Koops		1967	Barbara De Graaf Van Roekel
1953	Karen Mouw De Haan		1968	Kathy Oolman
1954	Ruth Oordt Strozdas		1969	Patti Roggen
1955	Joan Te Paske Mark		1970	Dawn Swets

"Pride of the Dutchmen" Band—Maurice-Orange City Schools.

Dutch Folk Dances.

116

Stage scene from Victor Herbert's "Sweethearts".

Queen ShirLee Vogelaar & ATTeNDANTS
1956 Tulip Festival, OraNge City, Iowa

Left to Right: Dr. Edward Fisher, Dr. H. J. VandeWaa, Henry Te Paske, Herman Moret, Dr. Wm Doornink, Mrs. James Treneman, Mrs. H. J. VandeWaa, Mrs. Edward Fisher, Mrs. Harry Dykstra, T. E. Klay.

DE SCHUTTERS

De Schutters were an informal organization established to support and promote the Tulip Festival in Orange City.

The group was organized in 1937 and held its first meeting at the home of Mr. and Mrs. Neal Spaan. Edward Bolluyt was named leader and director, and James Treneman was the piano accompanist.

The membership in De Schutters included Doctor and Mrs. William Doornink, Doctor and Mrs. Edward Fisher, Doctor and Mrs. H.J. Vande Waa, Mr. and Mrs. T.E. Klay, Mr. and Mrs. Harry Dykstra, Mr. and Mrs. Edward Bolluyt, Mr. and Mrs. Neal Spaan, Mr. and Mrs. Henry J. TePaske

Mr. and Mrs. Gerrit Noteboom, Mr. and Mrs. Herman Moret, Mr. and Mrs. James Treneman, and Mr. and Mrs. Elmer Doornink.

De Schutters held meetings during the late winter and early spring of each year to learn the Dutch songs which were sung by the group.

For many years De Schutters built a boat about 36 feet long and mounted it on the chassis of a lumber truck. The boat was one of the featured units in the Tulip Festival parades. The members, dressed in Dutch costumes, rode in the boat and sang the Dutch songs along the parade route.

De Schutters also took their boat to neighboring towns and cities to promote and develop interest in the Tulip Festival.

Children Time

at

Tulip Time

OUR COMMUNITY

CITY GOVERNMENT

In September, 1869, seventy-five men in eighteen wagons with three surveyors and provisions moved into the Orange City area. On August 1, 1870, the group known as the Orange City Association filed the original plat, which included the area from Albany Avenue to Delaware Avenue, and Seventh Street north to Second Street south. In January, 1884, thirty-one of the 800 inhabitants filed a petition for incorporation of what now is known as Orange City, Iowa. On February 29, 1884, 116 cast ballots in the election with 72 voting yes and 44 voting no. The election results were then published in the Sioux County Herald, which was a weekly newspaper printed in Orange City.

The four original settlers were Leen van der Meer, Dirk Van Den Bos, Henry John vander Waa, and Henry Hospers. Like all Hollanders, the Dutch in the colony in Sioux County, forgetting the persecutions instigated by their Prince, prided themselves on being "Orange-men" (their ancestors being adherent to the House of Orange-Nassau, meaning "Orange forever") — and so they gave the title of the Dutch Royal House to their settlement calling it "Orange City".

They set aside one block for a public park, staked off lots and laid aside 1/5 of the proceeds of the sale from those lots, for a college fund. One of the first buildings was a school house, around which the town grew. Twelve years after they came to Sioux County they founded a church school, the Northwestern Classical Academy.

These Hollanders became a power at the poles, and the county seat was transferred from Calliope to Orange City. Henry Hospers, who had been instrumental in founding the colony, left Pella, where he had previously lived, and became the leading spirit in the young Dutch settlement. In his paper — "Little Friend of The People" (Devolks-vriend) he advertised the advantage of the locality, and attracted the attention of immigrants to the spot.

Orange City, Iowa was listed as a City instead of a Town in 1950 with a population of 2,166 at that time. The 1960 census showed a population of 2,707, and a special census taken in 1967 revealed the present population of 3,463.

Presently serving Orange City as Mayor is Robert Dunlop, and Councilmen include Gillis Haverdink, Nelson Muilenburg, Cornelius Siebersma, Roy Vander Stoep, and James Woudstra.

MAYOR ROBERT M. DUNLOP

ORANGE CITY MAYORS

Antonie J. Betten	1884 – 1885
Henry Hospers	1885 – 1887
H. Slikkerveer	1887 – 1888
A. Vander Meide	1888 – 1890
Wm Hutchinson	1890 – 1891
Wm F. Rieckhoff	1891
A. Bolks	1891 – 1895
Fred Slob	1895 – 1896
A. Bolks	1896 – 1902
P. D. Van Oosterhout	1902 – 1906
H. Slikkerveer	1906 – 1916
G. Klay	1916 – 1922
Cor. Van De Steeg	1922 – 1950
Arie Vander Stoep	1950 – 1958
Chester Van Peursum	1958 – 1964
Robert M. Dunlop	1964 –

ORANGE CITY UTILITIES

For a number of years after Orange City's incorporation, the people obtained their water from their own wells, or purchased it from the city well. Over the years, the feeling grew amongst the residents that the existing water supply system was not adequate for fire protection. In late 1895, the City Council took action to let the voters decide if the City should erect a waterworks system at the cost of $8500. Of the ballots cast, 114 people favored the proposal, 51 opposed it.

After rejecting the first set of bids submitted, the contract was awarded to Fairbanks Morse. And thus, the waterworks system became a municipal enterprise.

Board of Trustees
Orange City Municipal Utilities
Edward Schreur, Merlyn Kraai, Chairman, Franklin Vogel.

Left to right: H. C. Moret, City Treasurer; Don Schreur, City Clerk; Allen Roos, Utilities manager.

THE CITY COUNCIL

Left to right: Gillis Haverdink, Nelson Muilenburg, Cornelius Siebersma, James Woudstra, Roy Vander Stoep.

In the area of electric power, the residents of Orange City received their power from privately-owned companies until 1923. During 1922 sentiment arose that the private rates were too high and that the city should have its own electric plant. Again the Council permitted the voters to make the final decision. Interestingly enough, in this election the men and women were required to vote separately, and their votes were counted separately. The voters had to decide whether or not to erect a municipal electric light plant and the necessary transmission line within the town at a cost of $45,000. Voters were overwhelmingly in favor of the proposal; and, after Iowa Light Co. agreed to accept $10,000.00 for the entire distribution

system, bids were accepted for the remainder of the project. Fairbanks, Morse, and Co. was awarded the contract for the line material. By late 1923, electric power was added to the municipal utility system.

The sanitary sewer system had no formal beginning but gradually evolved into the present municipal facility.

A special election held in 1959 placed all of these aspects of the municipal utility system under the control of a Board of Trustees. The Board presently consists of Merlyn Kraai, Franklin Vogel, Edward Schreur, with Allen Roos serving as Utilities Manager.

Planning and Zoning Commission
Standing, left to right: Calvin Groen, Donald Hop, John Ter Horst, Arthur Vogel.
Seated, left to right: Peter Blom, Lloyd Kepp, Chairman, William Top.

PLANNING AND ZONING COMMISSION

Soon after the close of World War II, Mayor Arie Vander Stoep and the City Council were keenly aware that Orange City was prospering and that it would be difficult for the City Council to keep pace with its growth.

In order that development would proceed in an orderly and systematic manner they deemed it wise for the city to have a Planning and Zoning Commission.

The Commission assists the Council in the development phase of planning, and makes recommendations to the City Council. In order to develop the city and to get the various branches of city government working toward a common goal, it was deemed necessary to have a definite plan for this development.

Through Federal assistance the commission developed a "comprehensive plan" for the city. The Commission is now responsible for the implementation of this plan.

Board of Adjustment and Appeals
Left to right: Paul Van Engelenhoven, Earl Bonnema, Orville Dorschner, Chairman, E. O. Lancaster, Clifford Bogaard.

Development Corporation Board of Directors
Back row, left to right: Earl Klay, Frank Vogel, John Ter Horst, Don Schreur, Clifford Bogaard, Franklin De Haan, Allen Roos.
Front row, left to right: John B. Draayer, Allen Faber, Director, Virgil Rowenhorst, President, Wally Luhrs, Paul Van Engelenhoven.

DEVELOPMENT CORPORATION

The Orange City Development Corporation was organized at a public meeting as a profit making corporation with the investors owning shares of stock. The capital thus produced was used to buy a total of some 190 acres of farm real property immediately adjacent upon the City of Orange City. In cooperation with the City of Orange City, the federal and state government, this property was improved with a municipal airport, leaving approximately 100 acres of highly improved "Air Park" industrial property. Eight 5-acre tracts were made available to industrial prospects and sold to them with or without improvements. A larger 40-acre tract was retained for larger industry. As the real property is paid for the return of capital and profits would be reinvested in other real property for further industrial development. There are approximately 50 shareholders, all residents of the City of Orange City, who actively work for the increase of the industrial base to the economy of the city. Since its organization the Development Corporation has located three new industrial enterprises within the city and has been of assistance to other industry already established. The organization is working constantly to continue to improve the industrial payroll of the city.

THE PARK BOARD

When the city of Orange City, Iowa, was first platted, one square block was set aside near the center of the city to be used for a public park. This park, now called Windmill Square, has been used exclusively as a public park since that time. Some years ago a band shell was built in the northwest corner of the park, and later a three stall fire station was added thereto. A windmill information booth is located in the southeast corner of the park; and during the annual tulip festival, this serves as an information booth and general festival headquarters. Adequate picnic tables and benches have been available for many years, and recently a picnic shelter house and some gas grills have been installed for the convenience of those who want to use the facilities of the park.

On November 1, 1939, a 20-acre tract of land was purchased from Mr. and Mrs. John Mason with the stipulation that the city was to pay to John Mason and his wife, or the survivor during the term of his natural life, the sum of $25 per month. This tract of land is presently known as Veterans Memorial Park, with a very fitting memorial to all veterans having been installed by the Pressman-Kosters Legion Post of Orange City during the year of 1966. The park presently contains a football practice field, a softball and baseball diamond, and the Orange City Municipal Utility electrical generating plant. There is also a Boy Scout shelter house, made possible in 1950 from funds given by the people in Orange City. One of the park's most popular features is a municipal swimming pool, built by the efforts of the Orange City volunteer fire department. Visitors also find a picnic shelterhouse, and a number of swings, slides, and other playground equipment available for the use of the children. A portion of the park is used for an outdoor ice-skating rink during the winter months. The Orange City Public High School formerly practiced football and played all of its games on the football field at the park. The Orange City baseball teams played all of their games on the baseball field, and presently the Orange City Church Softball League plays its home games on the softball field.

It is felt that more park space and recreational facilities are needed in a growing community like Orange City. After Orange City's general comprehensive plan was completed, it was evident that there were two or three ideal areas in the eastern part of Orange City, where adequate additional park facilities could be acquired. These areas are being closely surveyed in an effort to properly locate at least one other park site for additional recreation facilities.

Park Board Commissioners
Dale Boone, James Korver, E. O. Lancaster

The parks' recreational facilities are under control of a three-man park board. Presently serving on the board are James Korver, chairman, Edgar Lancaster, and Dale Boone.

DELCO BOARD
Standing, left to right: Virgil Rowenhorst, Robert Dunlop, Gillis Haverdink, Paul Van Engelenhoven, John Vermaat.
Seated, left to right: Allen Roos, Merlyn Kraai, Chairman, Allen Faber.

THE DELCO BOARD

The Delco Board was organized to provide some continuity between the various organizations promoting the orderly growth of Orange City.

Members of the Board are chosen from General City Government, Chamber of Commerce, Municipal Utilities, and the Industrial Development Corporation.

ORANGE CITY VOLUNTEER FIRE DEPARTMENT

Standing, left to right: John Vermaat, William Tolman, Martin Vander Broek, George Vande Kamp Jr., Jack Van Rooyan, Robert Newendorp, Calvin Groen, David Van Peursem, Don Schreur, Henry Jonker, Dennis Punt, Peter Jeltema, Raymond Van Pelt, Allen Roos, Stanley J. Van Otterloo, George Huizenga, John Vogel, Rudolph C. Grienke.

Seated, left to right: Engelbert Gesink, John Zeutenhorst, Robert Schott, Alfred L. Dykstra, Orville Beltman, Chief, and Edward Reinders.

FIRE DEPARTMENT

The first fire company in Orange City was known as the Orange City Hook and Ladder Company. Around the turn of the century, the name was changed to the Orange City Volunteer Fire Department. Some of the known early members at that time were: H. Muilenburg, H. Nevenhoff, G. Pas, H. Tott, J. A. Brink, H. Ver Schoor, H. De Haan, Isaac Vos, William Betten, Issac Steenwyk, A. Leynkeek, D. De Cook, J. R. Eerkes, Ed Kooyeman, J. Bos, J. Raak, John Den Hartog, G. Vos, G. Bolks, H. Rhynsburger, A. Groen, J. Vander Meer, S. Tinklenberg, J. V. Oolst, J. Vander Meide, J. Vande Brink, and H. De Gooyer.

Rules and regulations were somewhat similar to our present day laws. The members drew up their own constitution and by-laws which they followed. Members were fined if they did not attend meetings and drills. Today we abide by similar rules.

Possibly the biggest difference today, from our early fire department, was equipment. In early days their equipment consisted mainly of two pieces; a hose cart and ladder wagon. Usually this equipment was pulled to fires by the firemen. Lanterns were used for lights and whistles were used at the scene of a fire by officers for different duties to be performed. Ringing of the American Reformed Church bell was their fire call. Their equipment was stored in the old pump house behind the old Town Hall. The first known fire truck arrived in the year 1927.

AMBULANCE DRIVERS AND ATTENDANTS

Standing, left to right: Rudolph C. Grienke, David Vander Wel, John Vermaat, Cornelius Siebersma, George Vande Kamp Jr., Raymond Wielenga, Robert Newendorp, Alfred L. Dykstra, David Van Peursem, Don E. Schreur, Engelbert Gesink, Henry Jonker, Stanley J. Van Otterloo, Robert Schott, Edward Reinders, George Kleinhesselink, Red Cross Instructor, and George Huizenga.

Seated, left to right: John Zeutenhorst, Herman Oordt, Miss Grace Dekker, Miss Kathy Sands, Mrs. Henry Westra, Orville Beltman.

Firemen were active in civic affairs. Their big occasion was the July Fourth celebration. Each firemen had his own uniform for marching in parades. Equipment was decorated and pulled in the parades. Tournaments were held at the County Fair and neighboring towns.

One of the largest fires witnessed in early days was in 1903. Three buildings, belonging to J. H. Smidt, Gibson and Mouw Bros. were destroyed on main street. Several firemen were injured during that fire. Other major fires since then were: the Oelrich Elevator, date unknown, Orange City Livery Stable in 1918, the American Reformed Church in 1926, Hawkeye Hotel in 1932, Orange City Public School in 1947, Vogel Vande Brake and Legion Bowling Alley in 1953, and the Vogel Paint Factory in 1964.

Our fire department is still very active in civic affairs. In 1951, the firemen went around with petitions for a new fire station, which was later built. Every five years it sells memberships to farmers for protection. This money is used to buy equipment. In 1960 and 1961 it canvassed the town for another project, this time it collected money to build a modern swimming pool. In 1969, again it canvassed the town for money to buy and erect a new storm warning system, which it hopes to complete in 1970.

The men who served as Fire Chiefs were: P. R. Schaap, S. Tinklenburg, G. C. Pas, H. Newenhoff, Fred Michel, Jake Ypema, Clarence Balkema, Don Kraai, Ed Schreur, Roy Vander Stoep, Allan Roos, George Huizenga, and Orville Beltman.

In 1962 tragedy struck the department, Stanley Duven was killed in the line of duty at a fire.

Police Department
Alvin Van Berkum, Anthony J. Aberson, Chief of Police, Larry Hoekstra.

Secretaries of City Utilities Office
Miss Norma De Boer and Miss LuAnn Olson

William Faber
City Hall Custodian

Street Department Employees
Dick De Vries, Elmer Wiersma, Street Commissioner, Don Wichers, Gerrit Wm. Kosters.

Municipal Utilities Employees
Back row, left to right: Fred Dykstra, Lester Dykstra, Stanley Van Otterloo.
Front row, left to right: Dennis Netten, Rudy Grienke, Alton Vink, Ethan Vermeer.

LIBRARY BOARD

Back row, left to right:
Mrs. Robert Huibregtse, Wally Luhrs, Mrs. Lloyd Kepp, librarian, Donald Hop, Mrs. A. J. Vande Steeg.

Front row, left to right: Mrs. Leon Roggen, Vice President, Mrs. Henry Te Paske, President, Albert Heemstra, Sec'y-Treas.

THE PUBLIC LIBRARY

One of the first projects of the newly organized Women's Club in 1915 was to promote a new public library. The committee appointed in those days consisted of Mrs. Bertha Dykstra, chairman, Miss Minnie Oggel, Miss Anna Pas, Mrs. C. Hospers and Mrs. P. J. de Kruif.

The first location was in a small and inadequate room in the old town hall. About 1920 the library was moved to an old shack just west of the present new post office building.

In 1926 the Women's Club took the problem of the struggling library to the City Council and asked them to make it a city project and to be supported by a small tax levy. The Council approved and Mayor Vande Steeg appointed the first Board of Trustees. The location was moved to the council room in the Hawkeye Hotel. In 1933 the library moved into its present location in City Hall.

On June 11, 1926 the newly appointed library board held its first meeting with Mrs. A. J. Kolyn as president, Mrs. C. Vande Steeg as secretary and treasurer; and Mrs. P. D. Van Oosterhout, Mrs. Henry Giebink, Mrs. W. Reickhoff, Mr. Gerrit Klay and Mr. C. L. Barks as board members.

In 1917 Mrs. B. H. Vande Waa was appointed librarian and served until her death in 1955. In recent years the continued success and growth of the Orange City Public Library has been due largely to the outstanding efforts of Mrs. A. J. Van de Steeg who was librarian for ten years and to Mrs. Lloyd Kepp who is the present librarian.

The progress of the library has been continual. New departments have been added and older ones expanded. New facilities are constantly being added. The library is a member of the War Eagle Cooperative for North West Iowa and has access to their teletype and microfilms. Today there are 20,000 volumes in the library and it is not uncommon to circulate 6,000 or more units in a single month. There are libraries in Iowa with three times our tax budget that do not circulate as many books as the Orange City Library.

The following people should be remembered for long and devoted service: in the early days, Mrs. B. H. Vande Waa, Mrs. Minnie Oggel. Mrs. C. Hospers, and Mrs. C. Aue. Of later years: Mrs. W. L. Reickhoff, Mrs. A. J. Kolyn, Mrs. C. Vande Steeg, Mr. G. Klay and Mr. J. L. Schoep who was secretary-treasurer for many years; of the recent years: librarians Mrs. A. J. Vande Steeg and Mrs. L. Kepp and Mr. C. L. Barks, whose concern was the budget, and Mr. William Cambier.

The present board of directors consists of: Mrs. H. Te Paske, president; Mrs. L. Roggen, vice president, Mr. A. Heemstra, secretary-treasurer; Mrs. R. Huibregtse, Mrs. A. J. Van de Steeg, Mr. W. Luhrs and Mr. D. Hop as members. Mrs. L. Kepp is librarian.

Through the untiring efforts of the library board and interested patrons, the voters of Orange City have approved an $80,000.00 bond issue and as soon as federal funds are available construction will commence.

TULIP FESTIVAL STEERING COMMITTEE

Standing, left to right: Jim Doornink, Allen Faber, Merlyn Wallinga, Cornie Stegink, Willard Rowenhorst, Dale Boone, Paul Van Engelenhoven, Orville De Jong, Art Vogel.

Seated, left to right: Dick Deets, Stanley De Haan, Don Schreur, Chairman; Merlyn Kraai, Frank Hulsart.

CENTENNIAL COMMITTEE

Standing, left to right: Bernie Vander Aarde, Henry Rowenhorst, Don Schreur, Robert Dunlop, Dennis Punt, Allen Faber, Stanley De Haan.

Seated, left to right: Dr. Martin Vander Maaten Sr., Dr. A. J. Neumann, Merlyn Kraai, Chairman, Rev. Everett Van Engelenhoven, Rev. Robert Tjapkes, Merlyn Vander Broek.

CHAMBER OF COMMERCE BOARD OF DIRECTORS

Standing, left to right: Harvey Pluim, Merlyn Kraai, John Vermaat, Dick Van Gelder, Jim Doornink, Paul Van Engelenhoven, Wally Luhrs.
Seated. left to right: Allen Faber, Manager; Charles Surber, President, and Frank De Vries.

Records available show that the business men of Orange City, already, in the early days recognized the need of organized effort to best promote their business interest and to develop their city in a proper, orderly manner.

On July 9, 1907 the Orange City Commercial Club was organized with the following officers elected:

C. Hospers	President
M. Rhynsburger	Vice President
W. W. Schultz	Secretary
T. W. Meeker	Treasurer

At the next meeting one of the items of business refers to improving the general appearance of the city. Committees were appointed and charged with the responsibility to carry this out.

May this worthy ideal ever continue.

The early minutes were written in long hand. For convenience, in many instances, abbreviations were used — perhaps a forerunner of our present day initialed Government Bureau titles.

Today our cities are faced with automobile parking problems. Minutes of September 3, 1907 (Horse and Buggy Days) include a motion to authorize installation of hitching posts along the four sides of the City Square, (now Windmill Square).

Excerpts from minutes showing Early Day Interests:

Nov. 1907 — Committee appointed to solicit funds towards the purchase of band instruments.

Mar. 1908 — Recommend fire escapes for the Public School as a safety measure.

May 1908 — Attempts made to get a District G. A. R. meeting in Orange City.

May 1908 — Motion made to celebrate the 4th of July.

June 1908 — Hire L. O. Lohr as town band director at salary of $20.00 per month. Later increased to $30.00 per month. Gerrit Klay appointed as band treasurer.

Aug. 1908 — Amount needed for band instruments $625.10
Amount raised by solicitations — $605.50
Short of goal — $19.60.

The band instruments became the property of the Commercial Club and were later turned over to a Junior Band.

Band concerts were held in the City Park, during the summer months, on Saturday nights. A relaxing entertainment for Orange City shoppers during those early times.

Oct. 1908 — Sponsored a lecture course program.

June 1915 — Club decided to sponsor a baseball team.

Nov. 1915 — Contracted with Redpath Vawter Co.

Allan Faber
Secretary of the Chamber

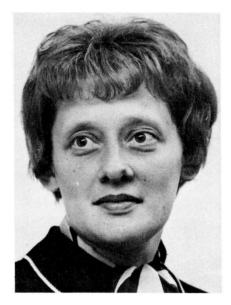

Mrs. Elmer J. Hofmeyer
Secretary for Chamber of Commerce Office

for a five day Chautauqua program for the summer of 1916.

Other projects supported were some of the following:

a. Support of a new hotel building.
b. Celebrate the 50th anniversary of this Dutch colony.
c. Support of Pioneer Memorial Home for the aged.
d. Support of Northwestern Junior College, later a 4 year college.
e. Many, many other projects.

About 1929 or 1930 interest in the Commercial Club seemed to be on the decline. A revival came about in 1936. The new organization was titled Chamber of Commerce. Articles of Incorporation for the new Chamber of Commerce are dated January 28, 1936.

Mr. G. J. Slobe became its first president.

A "corioddity" is that Mr. Slobe was a son-in-law of Mr. Hospers, the first president of the Commercial Club, as shown in minutes of July 9, 1907.

The Chamber of Commerce has been operative ever since and continues as of this date. It remains active in the promotion of business on Central Avenue (Main Street) and in its efforts to keep Orange City apace with a fast changing world.

In 1936 it sponsored the first Tulip Festival which has become one of Northwest Iowa's most recognized events. This year marks the 30th annual festival. During World War II the year 1942, no festival was held but one day was designated as a Government Bond Promotion Sale. No festival was held for the years of 1943, 1944, 1945 and 1946 in the light of concern towards the war effort.

As the Tulip Festival grew in size and importance it became necessary for the Chamber to appoint a permanent Tulip Festival steering committee. Upon this steering committee rests the responsibliity of each year's festival and this committee convenes at regular intervals during the entire year.

In the early years the secretary of the Chamber served on a gratis basis, but now with the increased work load of the secretary, a nominal wage is allowed.

The Chamber works in a cooperative effort with all city and civic organizations, and especially with the Orange City Development Corporation to induce new commercial firms and industries to locate in Orange City.

During the past two decades many changes have come about. Several new industries and commercial firms have located in or near Orange City. Several have selected the area near the new 2900 foot concrete airstrip to the south edge of Orange City.

The Chamber feels that Orange City has much to offer in the area of true, honest, American living. Its members are eager to contact any person, firm or industry who has an interest in locating here. The Chamber will be most happy to have you choose and claim Orange City as your residence.

Dedication of Sioux County Court House – 1904

THE COURT HOUSE

In 1859 four young adventurers from Sioux City, Iowa, went into new county organizing, at which they felt sure that they could hastily make a fortune. They chose Sioux County, Iowa, for their first venture. With camping outfit, drawn by mules, they ventured northward along the Sioux River until they were sure that they were within Sioux County. In the vicinity of what is now called Chatsworth, they constructed a dug-out and a horse stable, and returned to Sioux City for official papers from Woodbury County to which Sioux County belonged for judicial and taxation purposes.

The following spring they returned with authoritative papers to organize a new county. An election was held by the said four people, which constituted the entire known population of the county. The four elected themselves as county officers. The dug-out served as living quarters and Court House until

they built a new Court House further north, on lots laid out by them, as a new townsite, and they named the new county seat Calliope. The county officers voted themselves bonds for the construction of a new log-cabin Court House and for bridges. After two years these four, whose only purpose was to become rich quickly legally or illegally, sold their entire interest in Sioux County for a large sum of money to two new adventurers of similar character. The new purchasers, because of fear for the Indians, deserted the county for two years. Afterward, bogus county officers were appointed, including a board of supervisors.

Contracts for the construction of imaginary buildings, schools, roads, and bridges were let at extravagant prices. Chicago brokers sold the fraud - ulent bonds for some $200,000. leaving the county in debt to that amount with nothing to show for it

134

First Sioux County Court House–1904

except a log-cabin Court House and a few fake bridges across the later called Six-Mile Creek and Dry Creek.

The county government a Calliope, disregarding the law handled matters according to their own personal interests.

The new settlers, chiefly of dutch descent, in the eastern part of Sioux County, disapproved of the unlawful manner in which the county official business was being conducted. This was proven by the eastern settlers who insisted on honest government. At the election in the fall of 1871 a new slate of officers was elected, with only Henry Hospers re-elected as member of the board of supervisors.

On January 1, 1872, all the newly-elected officers were sworn in except the auditor and treasurer, because the Calliope group claimed that the bonds of the auditor and treasurer were insufficient and illegal. The two rejected elected officers returned a few days later and guaranteed to do anything within in reason to correct any pretended insufficiency. The board refused again. Thereupon the eastern settlers decided to go to Calliope enmasse and try to settle the matter in a friendly manner.

On a cold January 22, 1872, morning a cavalcade of some 55 bob sleighs from the eastern part of the county and from the Rock Valley, Hull, and other territories descended upon the town of Calliope. The board of supervisors was in session. Consternation seized them, and the board hastily adjourned. The group informed the sheriff that they had come to see to it that the duly-elected officers were installed. If this was done, there would be no trouble. Preventing the chairman of the board to to hitch his horse to the buggy, he escaped into South Dakota on horseback.

Among the group was attorney Pendelton from Sioux City, whom the raiders had engaged as their legal advisor. The remaining leaders of the Calliope officers were informed that if the duly elected auditor and treasurer were installed immediately there would be no trouble. They replied "No gang of wooden-shoe dutchmen will run this county." Then Mr. Pendleton, after additional pleading, exclaimed "I can do no more; it is up to you boys." Thereafter, the men proceeded by force to enter the court house, removed the large safe and placed it on the bob sled, removed the books from the offices, and transported all to temporary buildings in Orange City.

A few days later an officer from Calliope came to Orange City advising that the bonds of the newly auditor and treasurer would be accepted if the safe and records would be returned. The eastern leaders accepted this offer, and the safe and official records were promptly returned to Calliope. The bonds, however, were voluntarily reduced from the excessive amount of $50,000 to $10,000.

The easterners, wishing to proceed legally, circulated petitions which were granted by the board of supervisors to call an election to re-locate the court house from Calliope to Orange City. The election, after due notice, was held in November, 1872. There were 250 votes cast for re-location to Orange City and 65 votes for remaining in Calliope.

In the beginning of 1873 the county government, the safe, and records were transferred to Orange City. A hastily constructed shack was built to serve as a court house. Soon afterward a frame court house was constructed in the center of the present Orange City park. This building served until it was replaced in 1904 by the present court house.

It is remarkable that the people of Hawarden harbored no ill feeling or disrespect toward Orange City because of that episode. On the contrary people such as Walter Scott, Bayard French, the Slifes, the Lunotts, the Sedgwicks, the Shoemakers, the Westergards, the Johnsons, the Gearharts, the Brunskills, and many others of similar purpose showed high respect for Orange City.

The court house, with its lofty tower crowned by the statue of justice, stands in the midst of the court house square where colorful tulips adorn its lawn. On the west wall of the main floor hang painted portraits of the four original pioneers. On the opposite wall hangs a painting of the covered wagon and the span of mules, with the four original pioneers standing beside the wagon. A large lighted bronze tablet showing the ten commandments hangs from the south wall.

M. J. Van Wyk
Sioux County Auditor

Stanley L. De Haan
Sioux County Treasurer

Mrs. Alice Van Roekel
Sioux County Recorder

Clerk of Courts, Mr. Olin G. Reiniger, and his deputy.

Merlyn Vander Broek
Sioux County Clerk of District Court

W. K. Price
Sioux County Superintendent
of Schools

Ted Hoogland
Sioux County Sheriff

Mr. Dick Wissink, County Auditor, and Deputy Herman Te Paske. Herman Te Paske was Henry's father.

137

Orville Dorschner
Sioux County Engineer

Willis Meylink
Sioux County Assessor

Mrs. Bernice Bergsma
Sioux County Nurse

Mrs. Jo De Haan
Executive Secretary Sioux County
Selective Service

Robert Huibregtse
Sioux County Attorney

William Berry
Director of Sioux County Board of
Social Service

Gerrit J. Brands, President   *Alden Walraven*   *Henry J. Wissink*

SIOUX COUNTY BOARD OF SUPERVISORS

Vern Mallette   *Simon Scholten*

The Court House 1970

Marion L. Jensen
Sioux County Steward

Dorothy Jensen
Sioux County Matron

The County Home

The Post Office Grows With Orange City

Items from Sioux County Herald:

10/11/72 Henry Hospers sells out dry goods & grocery store to Kuyper Bros. Post Office in this store.

2/21/73 H. Hospers resigns as Postmaster and Simon Kuyper appointed.

2/12/74 Postmaster can now accommodate those wishing to send money by registered mail. Charges are 8¢ per letter instead of 15¢ as before.

2/12/74 A petition is being circulated to get a much needed Post Office at East Orange, Alton.

Feb. 5/74 G. Dingman bought house, lot and barn from N Jongewaard near the Postoffice and also the mail route and carrying privilege between Orange City and East Orange.

4/20/76 Herald cries loudly for a radical reform in the arrival of our mail from the station. Mail comes in at 2:30 A.M. and we have to wait until 9:30 or 10:00 in the morning. It should be here at 7:30.

Old Post Office—Pictured left to right: Ben Kempers, Carrier; Oke Herwynan, Carrier; John Brolsma, Postmaster; Ed Fisher, Carrier.

*Orange Cuty's new **federal postoffice building erected in 1968**. Del De Haan, postmaster*

May It Please The Court

P. D. Van Oosterhout

Ever since the forceable removal of the county government of Sioux County from Calliope to Orange City on January 22, 1872, Orange City has been well represented by a succession of capable lawyers. There are presently seven attorneys practicing in Orange City. Henry J. Te Paske, Gerrit L. Rens and John D. Te Paske are associated in the firm of Te Paske and Rens, and Earl T. Klay and Norman Bastemeyer are partners in the firm of Klay and Bastemeyer. Individual practice law offices are maintained by Cor. "Casey" Vande Steeg and by Robert Huibregtse.

Another native Orange Cityan, the honorable Martin D. Van Oosterhout practiced with his late father, P. D. Van Oosterhout, until his appoint-

ment as an Iowa District Court Judge in 1943. Twelve years later, Judge Van Oosterhout was appointed to the United States 8th Circuit Court of Appeals and he presently serves as Chief Judge of this court, which hears Federal Appellate cases in St. Louis.

Back before the turn of the century, when Sioux Center, Alton, and Maurice all were seeking to take the Sioux County Government away from Orange City, and when attorneys wore tails and silk hats, no less than eleven Orange City lawyers can be found mentioned in the official court records.

One of the earliest, Lammert Van Oolst, who practiced in the present Masonic Lodge above De Haan Electric disappeared while on a cattle buying

The Hon. Martin D. Van Oosterhout. Chief Justice United States Eighth District Court of Appeals. United States Court of Appeals. United States Court and Customs House, St. Louis, Missouri.

Lewis De Koster

Cor Van De Steeg

trip in 1900 and was never heard from again.

The firm of Pitts and Vander Meide was located in early Orange City, as was the partnership of Orr and TePaske, until Anthony TePaske left to begin his long practice in Sioux Center.

George T. Hatley, a colorful trial lawyer, and Charles Irwin started a law practice before 1900 that continues to this day under the able skills of Cor. Vande Steeg who joined Hatley in 1916 and has practiced law in Orange City ever since.

Pieter Dirk Van Oosterhout began his legal career, and the present firm of TePaske and Rens about 1894 by joining in partnership with William Hutchinson, a fine gentleman but poor marksman at the spittoon, who was soon appointed to the in-

fluential position of District Court Judge and was instrumental in keeping Orange City as the seat of the County Government.

After gaining experience for a couple of years with Hutchinson and Van Oosterhout, Gerrit Klay founded the present firm of Klay and Bastemeyer in 1898. Mr. Klay, who never did attend law school, was a widely respected trial lawyer. He was joined by his son Teunis E. "Deacon" Klay in 1915 and the two practiced together until the elder Klay's death in 1939.

By 1899 P. D. Van Oosterhout had joined forces with his brother in law, John W. Hospers, who practiced with him until he died suddenly at the age of thirty-six in 1914. At that time, Mr. Van Oos-

A. J. Kolyn

Robert R. Huibregtse

Attorneys Gerrit L. Rens, Henry J. Te Paske, John D. Te Paske

terhout took another brother-in-law, Andrew J. "Judd" Kolyn, into partnership in the firm. In addition to his brilliant legal skills, "Judd" Kolyn was an accomplished composer and musician who wrote and directed several Tulip Festival Musicals before his death in 1942.

Martin Van Oosterhout joined his father and uncle in the law practice in 1924. During his nineteen years with the firm he served several terms in the Iowa House of Representatives, before going on to his distinguished judicial career.

After practicing law in Sioux Center for eight years with his uncle, Anthony TePaske, Henry J. TePaske began serving his first of twenty-eight years as County Attorney of Sioux County in 1937. He

moved to Orange City, his native town and opened an office in the courthouse building until he joined the Van Oosterhout law firm when Martin Van Oosterhout was appointed to the bench in 1943.

After serving as Clerk of Court for a number of years, in the early twenties Olin G. Reininger, Sr., passed the bar exam and began practicing in Orange City. In 1936 he was joined by his son, Olin G. Reininger, Jr., who died of leukemia a year later. Gerrit L. Rens joined the firm in 1937, and in 1938, when Mr. Reininger, Sr., died, Lewis De Koster also joined the firm for a couple of years, and then continued the practice of law on his own, until his untimely death in 1962.

During the Thirties, Charles B. Hoeven, who

John W. Hospers

Gerrit and Effie Klay

Honorable T. E. and Effie Mae Klay

Earl T. and Mrs. Klay
Norman and Mrs. Bastemeyer

claimed Alton as his residence, was County Attorney and practiced law in Orange City for six years before he went on his long, and distinguished career in the Iowa Legislature and the United States House of Representatives.

In the late 1930's, LeRoy Van Der Wicken joined Cor. Vande Steeg in his law practice for several years until he left to take over his father's newspaper business in Grundy Center, Iowa.

After World War II, Gerrit L. Rens returned from Naval Duty and became the third partner in the firm of Van Oosterhout, TePaske and Rens, a partnership which continued until 1960 when P. D. Van Oosterhout's career as a great scholar and a gracious gentleman was ended by his death, at the age of eighty-eight years.

Also returning from overseas duty during the war, in 1947, Earl T. Klay became a partner with his father in the firm of Klay and Klay. After "Deacon" Klay was appointed an Iowa District Court Judge in 1955, a position he served with distinction until his death in 1963, Earl Klay practiced alone until native Orange Cityan, Norman Bastemeyer joined the firm in 1942.

In 1964, Robert Huibregtse became associated with the firm of TePaske and Rens for several years before he set up his own private practice on main street. John D. TePaske joined his father and Gerrit L. Rens in the law practice after graduating from law school in 1968.

Medical History

Strangely enough the medical history of Orange City begins in 1871 with the organization of the First Reformed Church in Orange City. In the spring of 1872 Rev. Seine Bolks of Zeeland, Michigan, accepted their call and became the first resident minister in Sioux County. He proved to be just the man needed for he also had a knowledge of medicine, obstetrics and surgery. He gave aid to the afflicted and injured without regard to religion, sect, or creed, and far and wide over Sioux County he was trusted, loved and admired. He was 58 years of age when he came in 1872 and died at the age of 80.

The first medical doctor in Sioux County was Dr. Edward O. Plumbe who came to Orange City in 1871. Because he could not speak the Dutch language he had difficulty communicating with the Orange City settlers and for that reason moved to Rock Valley in 1874 where he had a successful practise until 1907 when he moved to Chicago.

Dr. A. F. H. DeLespinesse was born in Holland in 1817 and had served as a physician in Holland for many years before moving to Orange City in 1873. He soon had a busy practise and also taught Latin and medicine to four young men who wished to become physicians. One of these was his oldest son who later became Dr. G. A. DeLespinesse. He continued to practise until his death in 1880.

Dr. Henry S. Baron came to Orange City in 1880 and was here during the smallpox epidemic of 1880-1881. An itinerant worker on the Chicago Northwestern Railroad became ill and Dr. Baron recognized this as smallpox. The patient was put to bed in a church stable as no one would allow him in their home. He died the following day. However, many people had been exposed and soon the epidemic was in full swing. Vaccine was obtained from the East but many opposed vaccination as they felt it thwarted the power of God, and they refused to be vaccinated. The epidemic became worse and many people died. Neighboring towns placed armed guards at their borders and no one from Orange City was allowed to enter. One history records that even trains refused to stop and went through town like the proverbial "Bat out of H--l." The epidemic was over in 1882 but Dr. Baron had become discouraged and moved to Pella, Iowa.

Dr. A. F. H. De Lespinesse

Dr. G. A. F. De Lespinesse

After the death of Dr. A. F. H. DeLespinesse, the people of Orange City asked his son, Dr. G. A. F. DeLespinesse, to take over his father's practise. He moved to Orange City in 1880 and was joined by his younger brother, Dr. A. F. Henry DeLespinesse in 1901. Dr. G. A. F. died in 1910 at the age of ninety years.

Dr. Carl Wormser was a quiet, dedicated physician who practised in Orange City from 1883 to 1903 and died at the age of forty seven. Dr. Heldering was a Homepathic physician from the Netherlands, who practised in Orange City from 1886 to 1888.

Dr. Albert DeBey came to Alton, Iowa in 1888 and moved to Orange City in 1890. He was a large man, weighing about 300 pounds. He was well-read, had a fine baritone voice and loved to sing. He played the piano and cello and belonged to a local orchestra. He was interested in politics and public affairs and because of his interest in surgery, he opened a small hospital in 1905. This was located across the street from the present hospital and just east of the present Medical Clinic. He was the first Sioux County doctor to perform major surgery. He

retired in 1933 and died in 1937.

Dr. Johanna Droppers is Orange City's only woman physician. She practised with Dr. DeBey in 1893 and 1894 after which she moved to Wisconsin.

Dr. Herman D. Oggel practised with Dr. A. DeBey from 1900 to 1902 and then moved to Maurice where he had a successful practise for many years.

Dr. Conrad De Jong practised in Orange City from 1903 to 1912 and then moved to Sioux City.

Dr. John G. DeBey joined his father in practise in 1910 and carried on a large and successful practice until his death in 1944. Dr. DeBey was active in the community affairs. He was a charter member of the Lions Club and also a member of the Shrine in Sioux City.

Dr. C. Vernon Fisher was a native of Orange City who practised in Orange City from 1922 to 1926.

Dr. William Doornink was born in Sioux Center, Iowa and began his practise in Orange City in 1926. In 1927 he opened a small hospital and later moved to a hotel which he converted into a hospital. He enjoyed a large and successful practise but was

Dr. Henry S. Baron M.D.
(Was here during the terrible smallpox epidemic)

Dr. A. De Bey

forced to retire in 1953 because of heart trouble and died in 1954.

Dr. E. B. Grossmann came to Orange City in 1937 and became associated with Dr. John DeBey. He served in the U. S. Army, 1942-1945, and while in service his partner died.

Dr. Alexander Bushmer came to Orange City in 1944 to help carry on the vacant practises of Dr. DeBey and Grossmann. Upon Dr. Grossmann's return from service, they formed a partnership and are still practising together. A third partner, Dr. Roy Hassebroek, joined the group in 1958 and a fourth physician, Dr. Paul Vander Kooi, joined the group in 1968.

Dr. C. B. Murphy practised in Granville and then joined Dr. D. J. Gleysteen at Alton until Dr. Gleysteen's death in 1946. Since that time he has practised in Alton and has been an active member of the Orange City Medical Staff.

Dr. E. B. Grossmann, Jr. joined the Orange City medical community in November of 1969 after completing residency training in general surgery. He is now a board qualified general surgeon.

It is of interest to note that in the eighty years since the first doctor came to Sioux County, the practise of medicine has changed considerably. Transportation is faster and easier and many towns that at one time had two or three doctors now have none. Here in Sioux County, Boyden, Hull, Granville, Hospers, Maurice and Ireton are now without doctors. In 1922 there were twenty-one doctors in active practise in the county and now there are eleven. Home confinements are non-existant. Bed patients are usually cared for in the hospital, and house calls are greatly reduced.

The original hospital started by Dr. A. DeBey in 1905 was moved across to the present hospital location in 1920. This was then a wooden structure and contained about six beds. This was enlarged with a north wing being added in 1941. This was again enlarged to the south and east in 1947. Until 1958 the hospital was owned and operated by the doctors. However, in 1958 the town purchased the hospital, tore down the center wooden structure which was the original hospital and added a west wing. This brought the hospital to fifty four beds on two floors. We are now again faced with crowding and the need for new and larger facilities.

Dr. John G. De Bey

Dr. Conrad De Jong

Dr. William Doornink

Dr. Robert Zylinga

152

THE DOCTORS
Standing, left to right: R. J. Hassebroek, M.D.; P. Vander Kooi, M.D.; E. B. Grossmann Jr., M.D., General Surgeon.
Seated; E. B. Grossmann Sr., M.D.; C. B. Murphy, M.D.; A. Bushmer, M.D.

Louise Jansen 1915-1935

ORANGE CITY

REGISTERED

NURSES

Rita Schnee

Mrs. Kathy Bogaard Frerichs

Following are brief biographical sketches of the dedicated nurses that have cared for residents of Orange City when they became ill:

LOUISE JANSEN graduated from the Sioux Center High School in 1904. She later took nurses training at Saint Joseph Hospital in Sioux City, Iowa where she received her degree in 1915. She worked in the De Bey Hospital from 1918 until 1940 when she was compelled to discontinue because of failing health which caused her death in 1944.

TILLIE STERRENBERG (Mrs. Charles) graduated from Saint Joseph Hospital in Sioux City, Iowa, on October 1, 1915. She came directly to Orange City and served in the DeBey Hospital. Later, she worked in the Grossmann-DeBey Hospital. She has retired and lives in Orange City.

MARTHA SMIT KLEINHESSELINK graduated from the Hospital Nursing School in Iowa City in June, 1926. She came to Orange City in 1938 and began nursing in the hospital here. In 1946 she became a full-time night nurse. She still is employed part-time.

LEONA SMITH VANDER STOEP (Mrs. Arie) graduated from St. Mary's Hospital Training School at Grand Junction, Colorado, on May 2, 1923. She moved to Orange City in 1928 and accepted a position as surgical and obstetrical nurse for Dr. William Doornink. Later, she acted as Hospital Supervisor and continued as a private and general nurse until the hospital closed in 1951. She rounded out forty-two years of active nursing in Orange City and area hospitals in 1965.

EULYN MEIER OOLMAN graduated from St. Joseph Mercy Hospital in Sioux City in 1946. She has been employed by the Doornink and Grossmann Hospital and is at present nurse for the Maurice-Orange City Community School.

ORANGE CITY HOSPITAL – R. N.'s

Standing, left to right: Mrs. Betty Johnson, R.N.; Mrs. Lois De Haan, R.N.; Mrs. Helen Van Gelder, R.N.; Administrator; Mrs. Eulyn Oolman, R.N.
Seated: Mrs. Martha Kleinhesselink, R.N.; Miss Emma Schnee, R.N.; Mrs. Matilda Sterrenberg, R.N.

BETTY SEGGERMAN JOHNSON of Marcus, Iowa, graduated from St. Joseph Mercy Hospital in Sioux City, Iowa, in 1947 and was employed by the Grossmann Hospital. At present she is employed by the Orange City Municipal Hospital.

KATHLEEN BOGAARD FRERICKS graduated from St. Joseph Hospital in Sioux City, Iowa, in 1952 and worked for the Grossmann Hospital. Later she worked in the Medical Clinic in Orange City until 1964.

RITA SCHNEE, Alton, Iowa, graduated from Sacred Heart Hospital, LeMars, Iowa, in 1930. She served as private and general nurse in this area from 1930-1937. In 1941 she was employed by the Doornink Hospital and she remained there until it closed in 1951. She continued to work in this area until her retirement because of ill health in 1962.

EMMA SCHNEE graduated from Sacred Heart Hospital, LeMars, Iowa, in 1930, She served as private and general nurse until 1936; then she came to Orange City. While living here, she has worked at the Doornink Hospital, for Dr. Zeilenga and Dr. Van Eldik as an office assistant, and for the Grossmann Hospital. Since August, 1959, she has been employed by the Medical Clinic here in Orange City.

LOIS ROWENHORST DE HAAN graduated from Methodist Hospital in Sioux City in 1947 and then was employed by the Grossmann Hospital here in Orange City. Later, she worked as college nurse for Northwestern College, at the Heritage House Nursing Home, and at present at the Municipal Hospital.

Clinic Personnel

Standing, left to right: Mrs. Beverly Rohrs, L.P.N.; Miss Joan Ver Steeg, Bookkeeper; Mrs. Retha De Boer, R.N.

Seated: Miss Emma Schnee, R.N.; Mrs. Mildred Vander Maten, assistant bookkeeper; Miss Ann Van Beek, Labratory assistant.

The Clinic

Old De Bey Hospital

Municipal Hospital History

Early medical care in pioneer days was of uncertain quality. The first doctor in Orange City arrived in 1871, a Dr. Edward O. Plumbe. His qualifications were dubious and his medical degree probably self conferred. Another pioneer medical man was a minister, Dominie Seine Bolks, who had had no formal training. Your choice of practioneers was, therefor, limited, unless you preferred an Indian witch doctor. However, they were not always available, frequently unfriendly and not fluent in the Dutch language.

The first qualified physician arrived in 1880, Dr. A. F. H. De Lespinesse. His son, Dr. G. A. F. De Lespinesse, came to Orange City to take over his deceased father's practise and was later joined by another son, Dr. A. F. Henry De Lespinesse.

Since there were no hospitals most of the early physicians made house calls and had small surgeries in their homes. Some of these early doctors were Drs. Baron, Wormser, Heldering, Stott and De Jong.

In 1890, Dr. Albert De Bey, a graduate of Rush Medical College, established his practise here and son, Dr. John De Bey, became his partner in 1910.

They found it impractical to treat many of their patients in a surgery and in 1906 established a six bed hospital in a residential dwelling. From time to time this was enlarged but while a great step forward medically it was a far cry from a modern hospital.

When Dr. William Doornink opened his practise in Orange City in 1926, he also established a small

Municipal Hospital Board
Left to right: Herman C. Moret, Amos Van Etten, Chairman, Robert L. Rieckhoff.

Hospital Ancillary Department
Standing, left to right: Mrs. Edith Olson, laundry; Mrs. Sadie Kosters, housekeeping; Miss Clara Bergsma, housekeeping.
Seated, left to right: Mrs. Esther Faber, laundry; Mr. Herman Oordt, maintenance; Mrs. Henrietta Zigtema, laundry.

Hospital Ancillary Department

Standing, left to right: Mrs. Loretta Hegeman, office; Miss Nell Huisman, office; Mrs. Esther Visser, office; Miss Barbara Swets, office; Mrs. Janice Nugtern. medical records; Miss LeAnn Huizenga, laboratory and x-ray; Miss Helen Hofland, office; Miss Geneva Feenstra, laboratory and x-ray.

Seated, left to right: Mrs. Ruth Sill, medical records; Mrs. Evadeane Klinghagen, R.N., physical therapy; Miss Joan Roghair, office manager; Miss Kathy Sand, laboratory and x-ray supervisor.

Nurses Aides

Back row, left to right: Mrs. Marge Reinders, Mrs. Rena Van Dyke, Mrs. Henrietta Vander Weerd, Miss Grace Dekker, Mrs. Kate Te Grotenhuis, Mrs. Marilyn Cooper, Miss Darlene Rehfeldt.

Middle row, left to right: Mrs. Sadie Ver Steeg, Mrs. Alice De Goei, Mrs. Phyllis Van Wyke, Mrs. Mary Mai, Mrs. Carolyn Horkey, Miss Marvella Dykstra, Miss Bertha Haverhals, Miss Barbara Heunink.

Front row, left to right: Mrs. Minerva Van Peursem, Mrs. Joyce Postma, Miss Judy Tjapkes, Mrs. Alyda Dekker, Mrs. Clarine Westra, Miss Beverly Kroeze.

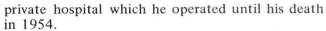

private hospital which he operated until his death in 1954.

Drs. E. B. Grossmann Sr. and Alexander Bushmer, both associated with the De Bey Hospital purchased the buildings and contents and enlarged and renovated it greatly. They operated it as a private hospital until 1959 as the Grossmann Hospital when it was sold to the Orange City Hospital Association.

Federal and state regulations were becoming increasingly stringent and it was apparent that private hospitals were doomed. The Orange City Hospital Association, a non-profit corporation, was formed in 1955 to study the possibility of building a new hospital. The Association elected the late George Dunlop as president and surveys were begun.

It soon became clear that raising money for a completely new facility was impossible because of the $900,000.00 estimated cost. Other avenues of approach were considered and it was decided to purchase the Grossmann Hospital and enlarge and completely renovate it.

After the Association had made several intensive fund raising drives, covering a period of three years,

$240,000 had been raised in cash and pledges. This and the proceeds from a $100,000.00 bond issue voted by Orange City was sufficient to begin work in earnest. The three hospital trustees elected on February 25, 1958 H. C. Moret, K. L. Seliger and A. D. Van Etten were invaluable in their help to the association.

Some of the many initial transactions which the Trustees and Association concurred in were:

Executed a ninety nine year lease with the First Reformed Church of Orange City for a fifteen foot strip of land immediately east of the hospital.

Purchased three residence properties to the west which were owned by Miss Joanna Harmelink, Miss Gertrude E. Dykstra, and one from Dr. Ted De Vries for a sum slightly over $20,000.00.

Contracted to purchase the Grossmann Hospital, which had been appraised at $69,500.00 from Drs. Grossmann and Bushmer for $52,-000, which included all equipment and contents.

The Nurses

Back row, left to right: Mrs. Florence Hudson, R.N., Mrs. Mathilda Sterrenburg, R.N., Mrs. Freda Bloemendaal, R.N., Mrs. Jeanette Waanders, R.N., O.R. supervisor, Mrs. Betty Johnson, R.N., Mrs. Evonne Jonker, R.N., Miss Joyce Vande Kieft, R.N., Miss Karen Nieuwsma, R.N., Miss Judy Wierda, L.P.N., Mrs. Rosemary Meis, R.N.

Front row, left to right: Mrs. Lois De Haan, R.N., Mrs. Jane Even, R.N., Mrs. Grace Toering, R.N., Mrs. Linda Egdorf, R.N., Director of Nurses, Mrs. Martha Kleinhesselink, R.N., Mrs. Helen Van Gelder, R.N., Administrator, Mrs. Bernadine Zigtema, R.N., Director of Inservice.

Hospital Kitchen Employees

Standing, left to right: Mrs. Verna De Kock, Miss Margaret Penning, Head Cook; Mrs. Minnie Eilks, Mrs. Dorothy Te Grotenhuis, Mrs. Ada Van Grouw, Mrs. Gertrude Van Maanen, Julia Bouma.

Seated. left to right: Maria Zaldivar, Millie Ver Steeg, Mrs. Eva Budden, Mrs. Mary Meis.

On August 7, 1958 the final plans were submitted to the Town Council for approval and on September 4, 1958, the General Contract was awarded to W. A. Kepp and Sons of Orange City for $130,383; plumbing to Visser Bros. of Orange City for $65,895; Electrical to Franken Electric of Sioux Center for $19,477 and an elevator to Montgomery Elevator for $7,215.

During the transition period of remodeling all hospital services were continued. Upon completion the Hospital Association deeded their interest to the City of Orange City and the new modern fifty four bed facility became the Orange City Municipal Hospital.

The equipment and services have been continually upgraded, the active resident medical staff comprises six doctors, including a surgeon. The hospital recently received a highly coveted three year accreditation from the Iowa Joint Commission. The replacement cost of the present hospital would be at least $1,000,000.

All of this has been accomplished by the dedication with which everyone has performed their duties. The current administrator, Mrs. Helen Van Gelder, the medical staff, the unselfish efforts of over one hundred employees, the invaluable aid given by the Hospital Auxiliary and of course, the loyal support from Orange City and surrounding communities.

However, as medical needs of the community have grown and new health programs instituted the Municipal Hospital finds expansion is necessary. All departments, the laboratory, x-ray, physical therapy, pharmacy, outpatient, kitchen, laundry, business office, doctors and nurses lounges, storage and maintenance need more space. These needs are a necessity and with a growing patient load additional bed space is a must.

A community hospital expansion committee is studying the many problems and will make recommendations to the current elected hospital board of trustees: Amos Van Etten, president; H. C. Moret, treasurer, and Robert L. Rieckhoff, secretary. It is an interesting sidelight on dedication to note that two of the trustees, Mr. Van Etten and Mr. Moret, have served since the Orange City Municipal Hospital commenced operation in 1959.

Hospital Auxiliary Board

Top row, left to right: Mrs. Marion Wiersma, Mrs. Peter Raak, Chairman of Sewing Committee; Mrs. Wilbur De Jong, Mrs. Ivan Muilenburg, Mrs. Bert Gesink, Mrs. Ed Mitchell.

Bottom row, left to right: Mrs. Howard Hall, 2nd Vice President; Mrs. Harold Vander Laan, Secretary; Mrs. Gt. Geurink, Treasurer.

Not pictured: Mrs. Arabella Sipma, President; Mrs. Wayne Vernon, 1st Vice President; Mrs. Wm. Mulder, Receptionist; Mrs. Wm. Van Gorp, Sr., Sewer.

HISTORY OF THE ORANGE CITY MUNICIPAL HOSPITAL AUXILIARY

On July 7, 1960, five members of the Orange City Woman's Club held a meeting to formulate plans for having a Hospital Auxiliary. They were: Mrs. R. Troutman, Mrs. H. Reinders, Mrs. C. Sterrenberg, Mrs. L. Kepp and Mrs. L. Moir. Miss M. Hauck, the hospital administrator, met with the group and served as their advisor.

Several meetings were held to write the constitution and by-laws and to elect officers. Tentative officers elected to serve until such a time when a regular board was set up were as follows: President—Mrs. L. Moir; 1st Vice President—Mrs. H. Reinders; 2nd Vice President—Mrs. C. Sterrenberg; Secretary—Mrs. R. Troutman; Treasurer—Mrs. L. Kepp. Five women were also named to the Board of directors.

On August 30, 1960, a membership drive meeting was held which proved to be very successful resulting in 669 members. Plans were made to hold the first annual Bazaar in November of 1961.

Auxiliary projects for this first year included furnishings for the geriatrics department and an isolette for the nursery. The funds for the useful equipment that aids in the efficient operation of the hospital come from membership dues and the proceeds of the hospital Bazaar.

There are also several committees who have worked faithfully each year and they are listed as follows: Committee for the Christmas Party for the hospital staff, Doctors and Board members, Committee for the Annual meeting, Committee for Sewing and Mending.

During these past ten years much equipment and many services have been supplied by this energetic group of area women and they look forward to greater service in the future.

Orange City Baseball Association 1946—Top row, left to right: E. Smith, A. Dykstra, Bob Dunlop, Al De Haan, Bob Barks, Fred Brower, Paul Colenbrander, Ad Jacobs, Onno Jellema, Mert Kraai, M. J. Van Wyk, Don Kraai. Seated: H. Cammock, V. Dykstra, Dave Schreur, Chis Van Citters, Annabelle Heemstra, Aud. De Graaf, Ed Reinders, Ken De Jong. Batboys: Unknown, Norm Bastemeyer.

COMMUNITY GROUPS AND ORGANIZATIONS

JOHN C. PRESSMAN POST NO. 329

Our War Dead

World War I — John C. Pressman

World War II

Allen Kosters	John A. Vande Brake
Henry Anthony Kosters	Lloyd H. Vande Berge
Glenn H. Beyer	Herman T. Vander Laan
John M. Hubers	Willard E. Vander Maaten
Frederick Cooper	Arnold L. Vander Wilt
Calvin B. Postma	Herman Vander Wilt
Gerrit G. Gesink	Charles W. Van Gelder
Neal H. Jager	Donald E. Wassenaar
Gerrit A. Ter Horst	

The local Post of the American Legion was organized in 1919 following World War I. It was named in honor of John C. Pressman, the first Orange City World War I casualty.

The Post Charter is dated December 12, 1919. The Charter Members are as follows:

Chas. J. De Vries	Olin G. Reiniger
John H. May	George W. De Kraay
Harry Muilenburg	Henry Kanis
Elmer F. Oelrich	Ray Casjens
Hessel J. Van Eizenga	Dewey Wiersma
Arend F. Van Wechel	Harold J. De Jong
Charles K. Balkema	John Oolman
Walter J. Muilenburg	

It is mainly a service organization for servicemen of all Wars. All meetings are held in City Hall on a rent free basis.

At the close of World War II many returning servicemen joined with the American Legion Post.

In 1949 the name was changed to read, "Pressman-Kosters Post" thus also honoring the two brothers, Allen Kosters and Henry Anthony Kosters who paid the supreme sacrifice during World War II.

Each year on Memorial Day the Legion gathers at City Hall from there they march to West Lawn cemetery to pay tribute, honor and respect to all our War Dead.

AMERICAN LEGION OFFICERS

Standing, left to right: Fred Vander Weerd; Anthony Verdoorn, Finance Officer; William Kosters, Chaplain; Gerrit Wm. Kosters, Post Historian.
Seated: James Vlieger, Commander; Homer De Boer, Adjutant; Marion Vander Laan, Vice-Commander; Jake Vander Griend, Sergeant at Arms.

The present membership totals — 190.
Deceased of all Wars — 114.

We take great pride in our Legion organization and our hope is that through our feeble efforts we may pass on to the generations, noble ideals for service to God and our fellowman.

These names are also inscribed in granite at the lighted entrance to Veterans Memorial Park, which in 1967 was dedicated as a tribute to their memory Also Inscribed in granite is the following tribute: —

"We remember these who fought and died to keep our Country free. Let us, with the help of God, preserve our Liberty."
In fitting ceremony this Memorial was presented by the Legion Post to the City.

The Legion has a deep community interest and participates in many city and community activities.

One of the first benefits rendered to the community following World War II was to arrange for a four lane Bowling Alley. Andrew Vogel allowed installation of the alleys in the basement of his mercantile building on a 10 year rent free basis. This provided recreation for the Veterans and the public alike.

In 1953 this building was totally destroyed by fire and with it all the alleys and equipment.

Cooperative effort by Legion members and the community resulted in a new building with six lane facilities, three snooker tables and a restaurant, providing a favorite gathering place for young and old. The building is owned by the Legion Post and present day replacement cost would call for $45,000.00

It is impossible to list all of the benefits provided by the Legion but we name a few herewith:

1. Memorial Services on Memorial Day.
2. Issuance of a Friendship calendar annually.
3. Serving on Many Tulip Festival Committees.
4. Lead all parades with Color Guard.
5. Display flags on streets for all prominent events.
6. Aid all Veterans needing assistance.
7. Sponsor Summer Youth programs - including Little League Baseball.
8. Furnished playground equipment for City Parks.
9. Provided Hospital Beds and Wheel Chairs for Community use.
10. Blood Donor Programs.
11. Arrange each year for two boys to attend Boy's State.
12. Many, many other useful and worthwhile community services.

Legion Auxiliary Officers
Standing, left to right: Mrs. Frank De Vries, Assistant Secretary; Mrs. Robert Vis, Treasurer; Mrs. Cornelius Siebersma, Assistant Treasurer; Mrs. Marion Vander Laan, Chaplain.
Seated: Mrs. Abe Schiebout, Vice-President; Mrs. Kenneth Van Wechel, Unit President; Mrs. Martin Raak, Secretary.

AMERICAN LEGION AUXILIARY

The American Legion Auxiliary, Pressman Post No. 329 came into being March 12, 1922. It was named to conform with the local Legion title and honoring John C. Pressman, the first Orange City soldier to lose his life in World War I in France, August 10, 1918.

Forty ladies formed the original membership and it is of interest to note that the first dues were only fifty cents.

The original officers:

President	Mrs. R. C. Durrell
Secretary	Mrs. William G. Van Roekel
Treasurer	Miss Anna Pressman
Chaplain	Mrs. Albert Balkema
Historian	Mrs. Harold De Jong

The Auxiliary has assisted in many worthy community projects stressing in particular those beneficial to the Soldiers.

In 1949 the name "Kosters" was added to pay tribute to brothers Henry and Allen Kosters, the first World War II casualties from the community. Today the 62 members meet in homes and carry out programs of education, Americanism, Child Welfare, Rehabilitation and Poppies.

Special effort is directed towards equipment such as wheel chairs, hospital beds, and other sick room needs.

Each year since 1947 a young lass is selected for Hawkeye Girls State under Auxiliary sponsorship.

Hospitalized veterans and veterans' children are given much attention. One of the Auxiliary highlights comes in the fall when a special tea is held honoring "Gold Star Mothers and Wives".

Y.W.C.A. Officers
Standing, left to right: Mrs. Homer De Boer, World Fellow-
ship Chairman; Mrs. Gerald Kalsbeek, Public Affairs Chair-
man; Mrs. Donald Mouw, Historian; Mrs. Marion Vander
Laan, Advisor.
Seated: Mrs. Einor Eknes, Advisor; Mrs. Jack Van Rooyen,
Co-Vice-Chairman; Mrs. Howard Hop, President; Mrs. Law-
rence Korver, Co-Vice-Chairman.

Y.W.C.A.

The Y.W.C.A. unit of Orange City was organized
in November of 1947. The following composed the
fourteen Charter Members:

Mrs. Fred Brower	Mrs. J. R. Reinders
Mrs. J. W. De Haan	Mrs. Gerrit Rozeboom
Mrs. John De Blauw	Mrs. Rena Roetman
Mrs. Howard Duven	Mrs. William Schalekamp
Mrs. Will Huisman	Mrs. K. L. Seliger
Mrs. Clarence Jonker	Mrs. Adrian Vander Stoep
Mrs. T. E. Klay	Mrs. Ben Van De Waa

Mrs. Karl Seliger expressed great interest in the
Y.W. and the Y-Teens and gave her whole-hearted
effort to its organization and the continuance thereof. In appreciation, she was presented with a Silver
Service, on its tenth anniversary. Ill health now pre-
vents her active participation. Girls from Northwestern College and Maurice Orange City High
School largely comprize the membership. The organization gives itself to many fine community
projects and world wide causes.

The excellence of the Y.W.C.A. is expressed in
its noble purpose. "The Y.W.C.A. of the U.S.A., a
movement rooted in the Christian faith as known
in Jesus and nourished by the resources of that
faith, seeks, to respond to the barrier-breaking love
of God in this day. The association draws together
into responsible membership, women and girls, of
diverse experiences and faiths, that their lives may
be open to new understanding and deeper relation-
ships and that together they may join in the struggle
for peace and justice, freedom and dignity for all
people."

Senior Citizens Board
Left to right: Nick Bogaard, President; Martin Van Peursem,
Mrs. Jeane Luymes; Mrs. Edward Schreur, Secretary-Treas-
urer.

SENIOR CITIZENS SOCIETY

This group was first organized and sponsored by
the Orange City Y.W.C.A. in 1947; later the group
disbanded.

Mrs. Karl Seliger, one time Director of the Iowa
Town and Country Y.W.C.A., was responsible for
reorganizing the group when a few interested per-
sons met at her home on October 15, 1960. Of-
ficers of the newly formed society were: Mrs. Jeane
Lymes, President, Mr. Martin Van Peursem, Vice-
President, and Mrs. Ed (Esther) Schreur, Secretary-
Treasurer, Mr. Martin Van Peursem and Mr. Sam
Wiersma have served as president of the group;
present officers are: Mr. Nic Bogaard, President,
Mr. Jake Bonnecroy, Vice-President, and Mrs. Ed
Schreur, Secretary-Treasurer (also Y.W.C.A. representative). Meetings are held once a month, during
the afternoon, at the town hall. Programs are varied.
Anyone interested is welcome to attend meetings;
usually thirty-five or forty men and women are in
attendance.

The Senior Citizens is an active organization in
our community and definitely fills a social and
cultural need for all who attend.

Lion's Club — Board of Directors
Back row, left to right; Stanley De Haan, Secretary-Treasurer; Thomas Kohout; Merlyn Wallinga, Norman Boonstra.
Front row: Norman Bastemeyer, Third Vice-President; Paul Muyskens, President; Franklin Vogel, First Vice-President.
Not in picture: Charles Auchstetter, Second Vice-President.

THE LIONS CLUB

The Lions Club of Orange City observes its 40th anniversary this year (1970) while the City of Orange City has its Centennial Celebration.

The Lions Club was organized in Orange City February 24, 1930 after an organizer from Lions International came to Orange City with letters of introduction from friends in Sioux City Lions Club to Dr. John De Bey and C. L. Barks. He explained to them the purpose and operation of Lions International. They both recognized its benefits and decided to help organize a Lions Club. They furnished him a list of leaders in the community upon whom to call.

He obtained his objective, 20 charter members, which he reported as follows: John B. Balkema, postmaster; C. L. Barks, bank president; Rex B. Conn, county agent; Dr. J. G. De Bey, surgeon; W.

H. Hospers, farm loans; T. E. Klay, attorney; Andrew J. Kolyn, attorney; I. Le Cocq, Ford dealer; Wm Leggett, hotel; G. R. Mason, Ford parts J. E. Oggle, newspaper; Ivan Pas, cafe; T. J. Reeves, court clerk; O. N. Ross, abstracter; K. L. Seliger, county engineer; G. J. Slobe, State Bank cashier; A. J. Vande Steeg, dry goods; J. J. Van Eizenga, lumber; M. D. Van Oosterhout, attorney; C. C. Yelton, automobiles. Charter membership also included five members who joined before Charter Night, namely — H. Lubbers, pharmacist; Wm. Doornink, physician and surgeon; W. J. Cambier, Chevrolet dealer; Geo. Dunlop, life insurance; John Cambier, Chevrolet dealer.

Dr. John G. De Bey was the first president and on Charter Night, April 4, 1930 accepted the charter of the Orange City Lions Club. The Sioux

Lions Club—1935

Front row, left to right: John Balkema, *Robert Hyink, Dr. W. R. Meier, Hessel Van Eizenga, *W. S. Slagle, *O. N. Ross, Charles B. Hoeven, President, *Gerrit Slob, *John Oggel, *John Brouwer, *George Dunlop.

Back row, left to right: P. H. Van Horsen, *Judson Kolyn, *Arthur Vande Steeg, Herman Moret, *Dr. H. J. Vande Waa, *Harry Dykstra, *Henry Lubbers, *William Vander Meer (visitor and guest speaker. Chinese Missionary, and not a member of the club), *John Cambier, James T. Grotenhuis, Cor. Vande Steeg, Rev. Jacob G. Brouwer, Rev. Bert Brower, Martin D. Van Oosterhout, Dr. W. Vande Bos, *Dr. Edward Fisher, Karl L. Seliger. (*denotes deceased)

City and LeMars clubs were sponsors.

The motto of Lions is "We Serve". Every Lions Club must perform some community service. All Lions Clubs in Iowa have united in one major project of Sight Conservation including work for the Visually Handicapped. Orange City Lions participate and in addition have had the privilege of helping one of its members who is blind, Mr. Henry Vande Berg, secure his leader dogs and other benefits. He in turn has been a great inspiration by his faithful attendance and resilient spirit.

Other community services sponsored include: Boy Scouts, including the building of a new modern scouthouse; indoor fair; swimming pool; summer recreation program; community athletic banquets; tulip plantings; the First Tulip Day Festival; scoreboard for college athletic field; Dale Carnegie Course; winter clothing for college boys from Kenya, Africa; assistance to the needy and various other community services.

The Orange City Lions have shown their enthusiasm for Lionism by sponsoring or co-sponsoring new clubs at Paullina, Kingsley, Primghar, Akron, Ireton and Hull.

Lions International, founded by Mr. Melvin Jones in 1917, has become the largest service club in the world. As of September 30, 1969, it had 893,013 members in 23,531 clubs in 145 countries or geographical area of the world, and continues to grow.

The Orange City Lions Club now has 87 members. Its president for 1969 - 70 is Mr. Paul Muyskens. It has played an important part in the growth, development and improvement of Orange City.

Historical Society Board of Directors

Standing, left to right: Charles G. Sawyer, Wayne Stewart, Mrs. Art Vogel, Andrew Vogel, Charles B. Hoeven, Mrs. Martin Van Oosterhout, Mrs. Don Schreur, Mrs. Henry Jonker, Mrs. William Verdoorn, Dr. A. J. Neuman.
Seated: Mrs. Lorenz Mouw, Assistant Treasurer; Mrs. Jim Doornink, Secretary; Mrs. Lloyd Moir, President; Bernie Vander Aarde, Vice-President; Dr. Martin Vander Maaten Sr., Treasurer; Reverend E. Van Engelehoven (not present for picture).

SIOUX COUNTY HISTORICAL SOCIETY

The Sioux County Historical Society was incorporated July 4, 1969.

Through the years, many individuals had voiced the thought that we should have a museum in Orange City, to have a place to keep the lovely antiques and heirlooms within the community and to retain early day history of the settling of Orange City and Sioux County. In late 1968, two individuals thought it was time to put words into action and have a Historical Society and Museum for the Orange City Centennial in May of 1970. Mrs. Lloyd Moir and Bernard Vander Aarde worked out some ideas and visited other museums and then presented their plans to the city council, and later to the county supervisors. They received their hearty personal approval and encouragement to proceed with their plans.

The first board elected included: Mrs. J. Doornink, Mrs. H. Jonker, Mrs. Lloyd Moir, Mrs. L. Mouw, Mrs. Jack Mouw, Mrs. Don Schreur, Mrs. M. Van Oosterhout, Mrs. W. Verdoorn, Mrs. Art Vogel, Dr. A. Neuman, Wayne Stewart, B. Vander Aarde, Dr. M. Vander Maaten, and Andrew Vogel, all of Orange City; L. V. Grooters, Boyden, Charles Hoeven, Alton, Mrs. A. Jurrians, Hospers, Charles Sawyer, Hull.

Elected as the first officers of the society: President, Mrs. Lloyd Moir; vice president, Bernard Vander Aarde; secretary, Mrs. J. Doornink; treasurer, Dr. M. Vander Maaten; assistant treasurer, Mrs. L. Mouw.

The Historical Society board has been busy this first year, setting up the membership drive, planning for a reprint of the "History of Sioux County" and holding a "Home for Christmas" tour of homes in Orange City and Alton. An old school house has been purchased and moved into Orange City, restored and furnished in the period of its day. The group is working closely with the Centennial committees to have large antique displays and demonstrations at various places. Several locations are being considered as a permanent location of the museum. All nationalities contributing to the settling of Sioux County will be represented within the museum, with the main theme being a Dutch motif to make it unique from other museums in the area.

Jaycees Officers
Left to right: Merlyn Vander Broek, Treasurer; Larry Den Hartog, Vice-President; Richard Deets, President; Marv Griepentrog, Vice-President. Ethan Vermeer, Secretary.

Saddle Club Board
Left to right: Arthur Ter Horst; Merle Van Klompenburg, Secretary-Treasurer; George Kleinhesselink, President; Arthur Kleinhesselink; Hallard De Jong.

THE JAYCEES

The Jaycees were chartered on November 21, 1964. They are "working together for a better community, state, nation and world".

CHARTER MEMBERS WERE

Keith De Haan	Dave Mick
Kent De Haan	Jim Nanninga
Don Hop	Bill Van Gorp
Dale Boone	Elwin Van Roekel
Jr. Siebersma	Bob De Geest
Bill Boote	Darwin Kots
Larry Den Hartog	Ed Doppenburg
Jay De Jong	Ken Schumacher
Jerry Ferrell	Darrel Roetman
Don Vander Stoep	Marv Zeutenhorst
Mark Gulick	Jim Aalberts
Dick Deets	Roger Mouw
Bob Huibregtse	Alan Vogel
Roger De Geest	Jim Welton
Marvin Vogel	Dave Van Wechel
Jay De Vries	Eugene Van Grouw
Al Van Abbema	Dennis Hansen

Many fine projects have been carried out by the Jaycees to make Orange City a better place in which to live, work and shop.

The Jaycees are made up of young men between the ages of 21 through 36 and truly are "Young Men of Action".

SADDLE CLUB

The Saber Saddle Club was organized on April 9, 1966. Six board members were elected as follows: David L. De Vries, President, Henry Visser, Vice President, Larry Ver Steeg, Treasurer, Jane Jonker, Secretary and Bernard De Jong and Norman Plender.

The purpose of the club is to encourage, promote and develop the owning, training, and breeding of range and pure blood horses, to promote and develop good horsemanship together with the knowledge and interest in the care, training and breeding of horses, to promote and cultivate equestrian games and sports.

The club is composed of approximately thirty-five members including single and family membership. Dues are five dollars for single members and fifteen dollars for families. Meetings are held on a five acre tract located one-half mile south of Orange City. Meetings are held every other Saturday from April through September and monthly during the winter months.

The club has ridden in parades of various celebrations, gone on several one day trail rides and also several overnight trail rides. The highlight of the year is the Horse Show conducted by the club members and sponsored by the local businessmen. Three shows have been held with an average of about 160 entries.

RAMBLERS

Back row, left to right: Dr. A. Bushmer, Frank Hulsart, W. K. Price, Mrs. Lars Granberg, Mrs. W. K. Price, Dr. Lars Granberg, Dr. E. B. Grossmann, Mrs. Gerrit L. Rens, William Cambier, Mrs. Frank Hulsart, Earl Klay, Mrs. William Cambier, Mrs. Lloyd Kepp, Mrs. Earl Klay, Lloyd Kepp, Mrs. Herman Moret, A. D. Van Etten, Herman Moret, Merlyn Kraai, Mrs. Harry England, Henry Te Paske, Mrs. Henry Te Paske, Robert Dunlop, Rev. Alvin Hook.

Seated, left to right: Mrs. A. Bushmer, Mrs. E. B. Grossmann, Mrs. Martin Van Oosterhout, Mrs. Cor. Vande Steeg, Cor. Vande Steeg, President; Gerrit L. Rens, Vice-President; Mrs. Robert Dunlop, Secretary-Treasurer; Mrs. Alvin Hook, Mrs. Merlyn Kraai, Mrs. A. D. Van Etten.

Ramblers not pictured: Judge Martin Van Oosterhout, Mr. and Mrs. C. L. Barks, Mr. and Mrs. Eugene Mulder.

THE ORANGE CITY RAMBLERS

On October 4, 1904, Mr. and Mrs. Philip Soulen, Mr. and Mrs. C. L. Wilcox, Mr. and Mrs. C. Hospers, and Mr. and Mrs. F. J. Lohr, in route to Hull, to watch a Hull - Orange City baseball game, a three hour drive by horse and buggy, stopped at a grove for a picnic lunch. There someone suggested that they organize a literary society for the winter months. The suggestion met with enthusiastic reception and the invitation to meet in a few days at the F. J. Lohr home was accepted.

At the meeting at the Lohr home, attended by the four couples and a few others, it was decided to meet again at the Wilcox home October 10, 1904, and to invite other couples by a notice in the Sioux County Herald to attend the meeting.

Mr. and Mrs. C. L. Wilcox, Mr. and Mrs. G. F. Dresselhuis, Mr. and Mrs. Philip Soulen, Mr. and Mrs. S. C. Huffman, Mr. and Mrs. Charles L. Dyke, Mr. and Mrs. Jno. E. Orr, Mr. and Mrs. A. DeBey, Mr. and Mrs. H. B. Morgan, Mr. and Mrs. C. Hospers, Mr. and Mrs. Geo. J. Bolks, Mr. and Mrs. F. J. Dohr Mr. and Mrs. P. J. De Kruif, Mr. and Mrs. J. P. Winter, and Mr. and Mrs. C. De Jong, attended this meeting. It was decided to organize a literary society, to meet at the homes of members and take up for discussion current subjects.

Later at the suggestion of Charles L. Dyke, the name of the Orange City Ramblers was adopted.

Mr. and Mrs. Charles L. Dyke, Mr. and Mrs. C. Hospers, and Mr. and Mrs. F. J. Lohr retained their membership all their life, the other charter members, except one or two moved away and surrendered their membership.

Meeting in the homes, the membership had to be restricted to not more than forty, and this membership is so prized that a very few ever resigned, unless they moved away, and forty and fifty year memberships are common.

They meet on Tuesday night about every other week, have two or three special parties each year, a picnic and a Christmas party. At the Christmas party they have a long established custom to "exchange" gift wrapped Christmas presents, each marked whether for a boy or girl, and to send these wrapped gifts to some orphanage.

This unique organization, unaffiliated with any other, is in its sixty-fifth year, has a membership of thirty-nine members, is presided over this year by Cornelius Van De Steeg, president, Gerrit Rens, vice president; and Mrs. Robert Dunlop, secretary-treasurer. Its membership includes a Chief Justice of the U. S. Circuit Court of Appeals, two doctors, a minister, a college president, four lawyers, a county superintendent, a high school superintendent, a college professor, R. E. A. manager, an undertaker, a bank vice president, a contractor, a couple of retired bankers, a retired businessman and a businessman. Each member is designated to participate in at least two items each year, present the program, entertain or act on a special "party committee", appointed by the annually elected officers at the first meeting each fall. In its sixty-five years it has continued its meetings uninterrupted and its membership is uniform.

The war-time constitutional limitation of coffee or tea and a sandwich following the program is consistently ignored by the hostesses.

SIOUX COUNTY CONCERT SERIES

Orange City throughout the 100 years of its existence has always offered a wide variety of good entertainment. The Orange City community has an undisputed reputation for the musical talent its inhabitants have produced throughout the years. This has been reflected particularly throughout the tulip festival and many other musicals that have been produced. Because of this deep interest in music, a number of individuals in the community felt this interest should be cultivated. The end result was the formation of the Sioux County Concert Series.

In March of 1956 a group of citizens met in the Trinity Reformed Church with a representative of the Allied Concert Services of Minneapolis, Minnesota. It was decided to organize a Concert Series. Rev. Charles Boonstra, pastor of Trinity Reformed Church, was elected chairman. Those who chartered the new enterprise with him were: Fred Roach, editor of the Sioux County Capital, Mrs. Agatha Te Paske Bolluyt, Dick Van Eldik, M. D., Mrs. Wayland Breese, Don Silvey, music instructor at the Orange City Public School, Mrs. Clifford Bogaard, Dr. Preston Stegenga, president of Northwestern College, Wilbur Ver Steeg, and Mrs. Carl Seliger.

The home of all the concerts throughout these years has been Northwestern College. The student body of Northwestern College participates on a 100% basis through their activity ticket.

The series began with a small budget and was sponsored largely by the local community. With the wide interest shown, it grew into an association that encompassed all of Sioux county and its surrounding area. Members from all the surrounding towns are now represented on the board of the Sioux County Concert Series. The budget has grown to a challenging sum.

Board members from Orange City for the 1970 season are: Norman Boonstra, president; Rev. R. Tjapkes, vice president; Albert Heemstra, secretary; Eugene Van Wyk, treasurer; Mrs. Clifford Bogaard, Mrs. Wayland Breese, Mrs. Stanley Duven, Eugene Mulder, Mrs. Robert Dunlop, Lawrence Van Wyk, and M. J. Van Wyk. Board members from the surrounding area are: Andrew Jurriaans, Hospers; John Vander Kerk, Rock Valley; Lucas De Koster, Hull; Mrs. Ivoran Noe, Hawarden; and John Wesselink, Sioux Center.

PIONEER HOME BOARD

Back row, left to right: Neal Dykhuizen; Henry J. Te Paske; Thomas J. De Jong; Nelson De Jong; Bernie Vander Aarde.

Front row: Jacob Hofmeyer, President; Mrs. Annette Bloemendaal; Albert Heemstra, Secretary-Treasurer.

Not in picture: John B. Draayer, Vice-President; Mrs. Gillis Haverdink; Mrs. H. J. Vande Waa.

THE PIONEER MEMORIAL HOME

The Pioneer Memorial Home, a non-profit organization, was organized and incorporated as a custodial home for the elderly on July 10, 1927. A board of twelve directors was named, with the following officers being elected: Samuel Muilenburg, president; John A. Muilenburg, vice president, Gerrit Klay, secretary, and G. J. Slobe, treasurer. Funds were solicited and a two story brick home was built and dedicated the same year.

Upon the resignation of Samuel Muilenburg, Mr. William Westra was elected as president and served in that capactiy for thirty eight years until his retirement in 1968.

In 1963, a new addition was added and opened for occupancy in the fall of that year.

Twice the operation of the home was disrupted, the first due to a minor fire, and the second as a result of the 1968 tornado, but in both instances, operations returned to normal after only a few days interruption. Thirty residents now occupy the home with Mr. and Mrs. Harold Kraai serving as stewart and matron.

172

Softball League Officers
Left to right: Merlyn Vander Broek, Secretary-Treasurer; Jack Van Rooyen, First Vice-President; Willard Rowenhorst, President; George Vande Kamp, Jr., Second Vice-President.

SOFTBALL LEAGUE

The Orange City Church Softball League was organized in May, 1956. The first officers were: Gerrit Mulder, president; Jack Ver Steeg, vice president, Stanley L. De Haan, secretary; Clifford D. Bogaard, treasurer.

At its beginning the league was composed of only six teams. This number varied from a high of twelve teams in 1967 to a ten-team league this year.

Admission to the games has always been on a donation basis. The proceeds have been donated to such worth while organizations as the Orange City Municipal Hospital, Church Missions, Northwestern College, and many others.

Woman's Club Officers Standing, left to right: Mrs. Maurice Eldridge, Mrs. Marvin Petroelje, Mrs. Henry Reinders.
Seated: Mrs. M.D. Van Oosterhout, Federation Committee Member; Mrs. Thomas Ten Hoeve; Mrs. James Doornink, Recording Sec'y; Mrs. Mildred Blumeyer, President; Mrs. John Vogel, 1st Vice-President; Mrs. Lars Granberg, Treasurer; Mrs. Herman Rowenhorst.

THE WOMAN'S CLUB

The Orange City Woman's Club was organized November 20, 1914 when a group of women met in the home of Mrs. A. J. Kolyn. Those present were: Mesdames Y. Dykstra, H. Rhynsburger, F. Fuller, P. J. De Kruif, F. J. Lohr, P. D. Van Oosterhout, W. Hospers, I. Hospers, H. W. Pietenpol, and Mrs. Kolyn.

The purpose of the club was three fold: Education, Culture and Civic Improvement. Through the years many projects were carried out. Some are listed below.

Education: Started and supported the library for eleven years; promoted the kindergarten, Girl Scouts, Boy Scouts, conservation of trees, summer recreational programs, dutch costume bazaars, supported the college, the museum, adventures in reading, bicycle safety program, presented sound equipment and movie screen to the city.

Culture: Promoted community Christmas Sings, teacher's receptions, poetry and art contests and exhibits, antique shows, flower shows, style shows, tulip festival activities, lyceum courses, Thanksgiving plays, teas for foreign students, musical teas, and film travelogue series.

Civic: Cleaned and landscaped public school grounds, donated refuse boxes on main street, benches for the park, playground equipment, encouraged the building of the community building, a tennis court, a skating rink, a swimming pool, assisted on rationing board of World War I, and with projects of World War II, sponsored the community chest.

The club reaches beyond the local community: it purchased towels hemmed by the blind women of Iowa, contributed care for Korea, presented gifts to residents of the county home and patients at Cherokee, veterans hospitals, Unesco, penny art fund, crippled children's campsite, I. F. W. C. president's scholarship, far east scholarship, international scholarship, and scholarship and loan fund.

The Woman's Club has received many awards: in legislation, year books, poetry and art, and civic improvements. The greatest honor to the club was having one of our members, Mrs. Martin Van Oosterhout, become state president of the Iowa Federation in 1951. Mrs. Van Oosterhout is a member of the International General Federation.

The Woman's Club has five departments: applied arts, better homes, crafts and hobbies, garden, and literature.

The following women have been presidents of the club: Mesdames A. J. Kolyn, F. Fuller, A. De Bey, C. Vande Steeg, G. Dunlop, C. Barks, Y. Dykstra, J. Bailey, H. Rhynsburger, H. Synhorst, M. Van Oosterhout, E. Fisher, C. J. De Vries, C. Tye, A. Vande Steeg, R. Troutman, O. Kraemer, J. Reinders, L. Moir, S. Scorza and C. Brickwedel. Mrs. E. Blumeyer is the 1969 - 70 president.

From a modest beginning, the club has grown to a membership of one hundred and thirty-five members.

The 1970 officers shown above left to right are: Associate Patron—Ward Kepp; Associate Matron—Armarie Clark; Worthy Matron—Bette De Jong; Worthy Patron—Al Hancock. Second row: Warder—Ethel De Geest; Chaplain—Willoughby Reiniger; Organist—Elsie Hasselo; Conductress—Mary Stallbaum; Associate Conductress—Marie Keiser. Sentinel—Anthony Hasselo. Back Row: Treasurer—Louise Kepp; Electa—Sylvia Gulick; Martha—Nellie Egenes; Esther—Karen Boeyink; Ruth—Lynn Freriks; Adah—Dell Reinders; Secretary—Rachel Van Roekel. Not pictured. Marshal—Marian King.

THE ORDER OF THE EASTERN STAR

The Order of the Eastern Star was founded by renowned poet and author, Dr. Rob Morris. The ritual was compiled and published in 1867-1868. This was the beginning of the Order of the United States as well as internationally. There are now more than thirteen thousand chapters with three million members. The office of the General Grand Chapter is in Washington, D. C.; also the International Eastern Star Temple is in Washington.

The first meeting of Century Chapter No. 298, was held on December 21, 1900, at the Floyd Lodge Masonic Temple at Alton, Iowa. The first worthy patron was M. D. Gibbs and the first worthy matron was Clara C. Bowers. The date for meetings was set for Thursday on or before the full moon each month. This made it possible for members from Orange City to travel to Alton by horse and buggy. The chapter was moved to Orange City in 1937, but it still consisted of members of both towns.

The Order of Eastern Star sponsors many worthwhile projects. They maintain a beautiful home for elderly members who wish or need to make use of it. The first Eastern Star Home was dedicated in 1905 at Boone, Iowa. The Home was enlarged in 1925 and again in 1959. The residents do not pay fees nor rent.

The General Grand Chapter established the Eastern Star Training Awards for Religious Leadership (ESTARL) in October, 1952, at a meeting in Milwaukee. This program was adopted by the Iowa grand chapter in 1953 and has been continued ever since.

The purpose for establishing the ESTARL were to encourage able young persons to dedicate their lives to full time Christian service, to assist financially those who are already preparing for such service, and have shown the capacity to profit fully from this assistance.

Individual members are given the opportunity to contribute directly to this project. In 1968 ESTRAL grants were presented to thirty young men and women in Iowa. Since its existence in this state, approximately $127,400 has been awarded to 361 students.

FLYING CLUB

The Orange City Flying Club was organized in October, 1969, for the purpose of promoting general aviation in Orange City.

Active members are all licensed pilots while associate membership is open to anyone with an interest in aviation. Bob De Haan serves as chairman of the group.

FLYING DUTCHMEN
Standing, left to right: Martin Raak, Lorenz Mouw, David Vander Wel, Carl Mortenson, Don Wichers, Art Vogel, Ray Wielenga, Nick Gaul, Keith De Haan, Darwin Kots, Marvin Vogel, Allen Wichers, Ray Mick, Marvin Vander Wel.
Seated: Norman Bastemeyer, Bob Nolan, Franklin De Haan, President; Albert Hancock, Art Cragle, Earl Bonnema.

Floyd Lodge No. 537 Officers
Front row, left to right: Anthony Hasselo, Treasurer; Ward Kepp, Senior Warden; Norman Bastemeyer, Worshipful Master;
Mark Gulick, Junior Warden; Robert Van Roekel, Secretary.
Back row: Herman Stallbaum, Tyler; Earl Clark, Senior Steward; Dennis Punt, Junior Steward; Robert De Geest, Senior
Deacon; C. Lee Barks, Chaplain; Lloyd De Geest, Junior Deacon.

FLOYD LODGE NO. 537, A.F. & A.M.

Upon the petition of Masons from the Orange City and Alton area, on July 16, 1894 the Grand Lodge of the State of Iowa granted a dispensation unto the newly created Floyd Lodge No. 537 to commence work. In its dispensation the Grand Lodge appointed the following officers for Floyd Lodge: M. D. Gibbs, Worshipful Master; L. D. Platt, Senior Warden; and L. P. Roberts, Junior Warden. In addition to the three appointed officers the charter members of Floyd Lodge were W. B. Richards, Secretary; Garret Bolks, Treasurer; H. J. Lenderink, Senior Deacon; H. J. Kamber, Junior Deacon; George Tauton, Tyler; M. E. Lewis and B. O. Blake, Stewards; William Hutchinson, C. D. Gidrick, Gerrit De Lespinesse, B. Schmidt, and W. J. Barrett. Charter member William Hutchinson was at that time serving as Deputy Grand Master of the Grand Lodge of Iowa and presided at the first meeting of the Lodge held September 14, 1894.

Floyd Lodge No. 537 met in Alton, Iowa, until it moved to its present location in Orange City, Iowa, in 1936. The Lodge meets regularly on the second Thursday evening of each month.

The present officers of the Lodge are: Norman Bastemeyer, Orange City, Worshipful Master; Ward Kepp, Orange City, Senior Warden; Mark Gulick, Orange City, Junior Warden; Robert Van Roekel, Alton, Secretary; Anthony Hasselo, Orange City, Treasurer; Robert De Geest, Orange City, Senior Deacon; Lloyd De Geest, Orange City, Junior Deacon; Earl Clark, Orange City, Senior Steward; Dennis Punt, Orange City, Junior Steward; Herman Stallbaum, Maurice, Tyler; and C. Lee Barks, Orange City, Chaplain.

ORANGE CITY - ALTON BUSINESS & PROFESSIONAL WOMEN'S CLUB

This club was organized March 3, 1955 by Angeline Kobberman, District Director, and was sponsored by the LeMars Business & Professional Women's Club. Elected at this meeting were Willa B. Reiniger, President; Naomi Ide, 1st Vice President; Mildred Hansen, 2nd Vice President; Mary Bowers, Recording Secretary; Wilma Klopfenstein, Corresponding Secretary; Betty Harbst, Treasurer.

A Charter Dinner was held April 18, 1955 at Orange City Town Hall, with twenty-six B.P.W. Club women of the district present, along with special guests. The charter was presented by Orlean Schroeder, State President, making the local Club a member of the state organization and federal organization. There were seventeen charter members from the two towns. Mayor Vander Stoep of Orange City and Mayor Aberson of Alton were present and welcomed members of the new club. Officers were installed by Vera Norman of the Sioux City B.P.W. Club.

Orange City-Alton P.B.W. Club meets monthly, usually at the homes of members. Many interesting programs on national and current affairs have been presented, often by guest speakers. The Club also has several social meetings a year, including summer picnics, and cookouts.

While the professed purpose of the national Federation is to promote the status of women, all local clubs are active in Community affairs. The Orange City-Alton Club for a number of years has paid transportation expenses of foreign students at Northwestern College to Des Moines for the annual State Association of Foreign Students convention. The Club has also sponsored collection of used and discarded eyeglasses for charity known as "Eyes for the Needy".

Present officers are Margaret Tiemersma, President; Mildred Blumeyer, Recording Secretary; Mary Bowers, Corresponding Secretary; Nelvina Scholten, Treasurer; Mildred Hansen, Project Chairman or Fund Raising Chairman.

Harry Kobes surveys beautiful trees, rock garden and pool from patio, all results of his own handiwork.

KOBES GARDENS

A visit to the Kobes Gardens from May until the nippy frosts of fall can prove to be an interesting experience.

Mr. and Mrs. Kobes acquired their acre in 1948 and with five years of diligent toil have converted it into the garden of their dreams. The greatest task was perhaps forming 100 tons of new rock into attractive patterns. The ornate, "Gateway to the Wishing Well", was at one time an altar in a Lutheran Church in Sioux City, Iowa, giving it an 1880 dating. Other rocks came from practically all the states and even a few came from foreign soil.

The Kobes register exhibits names from wide areas with many returning for another view of the Kobes creative ability. Flowers and hedges trimmed in manicured perfection, miniature water falls, with colored fish in the shimmering pool, warbling birds overhead make for serene outdoor living.

The Dutch Mill, driftwood area, and the refreshing patio scene supplemented with gracious hospitality are the visitors reward for stopping in.

Orange City is proud to have the Kobes Gardens located within its boundaries and with Mr. and Mrs. Kobes, Orange City says, "Call Again".

BOY SCOUTS OF AMERICA

Boy Scouts of America started in Orange City as Troop 208 in 1925. One of the early meeting places was 203½ Central Avenue in what is now the Masonic Lodge. The troop was started in the Sargent Floyd Area Council with area offices in Sioux City. In 1943 they transferred to the Prairie Gold Area Council with offices in Fort Dodge, Iowa.

In 1954 the present Scout Lodge, located in Veterans Memorial Park was built. This building was designed and built by Bernard Vander Aarde with the help of a number of local people who donated their time and labor. The slab and logs were hauled from Pine River, Minnesota, by Andrew Vogel, owner of Vogel Paint and Wax Company. The stone used in the fire place was hauled from the Floyd River area. Twelve or thirteen tons of rock were required to build the fireplace.

Rev. E. Van Engelenhoven was in charge of raising the necessary funds for the Scout House. When the $9,000 project was completed and paid there remained a balance of sixty cents. Our local Scout House is one of the finest in the state, and one we can truly be proud of. It was dedicated to Dr.

William Doornink, a local medical doctor, and a real Scout enthusiast.

Some of the local Scout leaders have been Elmer Doornink, brother of Dr. Doornink, Clarence Peters, and Milo Rhynsberger who was a full time Scouter for many years. Elmer Doornink was and still is very interested in Scouting, being a Scout executive in the state of Washington. Others include M. Van Roekel, Gerritt Rens, Arnold Dykstra, Mitch Moret, Wallace Hanson, and Darwin Van Gorp, an Eagle Scout who is presently a professional Scout employed as Director of Adult Training at Philmont Scout Ranch in northern New Mexico at Cimmarron. More recent Scoutmasters include Earl Klay, Virgil Rowenhorst, Bob Utech, Abe Schiebout, Cecil Keith, Orville Dorschner, Jim Doornink and the present Scoutmaster, Robert Schott.

Some of the early Scouts include Darwin Van Gorp, Robert Dunlop, Mert Kraai, and Robert Haverkamp who was one of the first Scouts to attain the rank of Eagle and is presently engaged in full time Scouting activities.

Present sponsor of the Scouts is the Lions Club which they assumed in 1930.

Boy Scout Committee
Standing, left to right: Lorenz Mouw, Publicity and Recruiting; Henry Jonker, Property; James Doornink, Institutional Representative; Charles Surber, Out'doors' Man.
Seated: Raymond Mick, Secretary-Treasurer; Howard Hop, Chairman; Marion Vander Laan, Advancement.

Boy Scout Masters
Left to right: C. Grienke, Dale Boone, Robert Schott, Donald Hop.

WASHINGTON ST., LOOKING SOUTH ORANGE CITY, IA.
(Publ. for De Kruif & Lubbers.)

TOTAL ASSETS

August 30, 1911.....................$	395,404.28
September 3, 1921.................	875,329.65
March 25, 1931......................	802,971.79
September 15, 1941	1,416,654.78
December 31, 1951	4,110,570.12
October 7, 1954.....................	5,181,658.02
December 31, 1959	5,259,167.24
December 31, 1964...............	8,485,828.81
December 31, 1969...............	15,129,138.13

The Business Community

NORTHWESTERN STATE BANK

For 88 years the Northwestern State Bank and the closely-related institutions which preceded it have provided Orange City and Sioux County with a complete banking service in the same convenient downtown location.

Orange City's first bank was organized in 1882 when Nels Kessey and G. W. Pitts of Decorah, Iowa, came here to launch the "Bank of Northwestern." The bank was located in the same general area now occupied by the bank.

Mr. W. S. Short entered the employ of the bank as a bookkeeper in 1884. Following the death of Mr. Nels Kessey, then president of the bank in 1883, and the sale of controlling interest by G. W. Pitts in 1904, Mr. Short was elected president of the Northwestern State Bank in 1905.

The Sioux County Savings Bank, which had been moved from Maurice to Orange City in 1935, was merged with the Northwestern State Bank of Orange City on September 23, 1937. The new organization was named simply "Northwestern State Bank of Orange City." The Maurice office was maintained and continues to be maintained as a part of the bank to this date.

Herman Rowenhorst, who had been president of the bank at Maurice from 1925 until the merger in 1937, became vice president of the new Northwestern State Bank and served as such until the retirement of Mr. Short in 1944. Mr. Herman Rowenhorst became president of the Northwestern State Bank in 1944 and served in that capacity until his resignation in January, 1965. He was succeeded as president by his son, H. V. Rowenhorst, who continues to serve as president to this date.

The success of this community bank, since the very beginning, has been in direct proportion to the successes of those whom the bank serves. As the people have been thrifty and have prospered in this rich land, the bank too, has grown in size and in services. It has always endeavored to aid the progress of this area. The formula for success which has guided the organization for 88 years can well be extended into the future—that men of character, who will save what they earn and add to those earnings by wise investments backed by their best efforts, are bound to succeed. The figures below summarize total assets over the last sixty years. These statistics are a measure of bank growth and of community development and are an index to the trends of the future.

W. S. Short

Herman Rowenhorst

Virgil Rowenhorst

OFFICERS

H. V. Rowenhorst, President
R. M. Dunlop, Vice President
Elmer Huizenga, Vice President
H. C. Moret, Vice President (Retired)
Marvin J. Grotenhuis, Cashier
Marion G. Wiersma, Assistant Vice President
Don Hop, Assistant Vice President
Edwin G. Doppenberg, Asssitant Cashier
Clifford Korver, Assistant Cashier
J. W. Holtdorf, Manager, Maurice Office

DIRECTORS

Clifford Bogaard
W. J. Cambier
R. M. Dunlop
Elmer Huizenga
Earl T. Klay
H. C. Moret
H. J. Te Paske
H. V. Rowenhorst
Franklin Vogel

EMPLOYEES

Angeline Vande Brake, Roger Brunsting, Donna Harmelink, Opal Hulsart, Adrian Jacobs, Sharon Kuyper, Inge Nagler, Jo Vander Steen, LeAnn Van Peursem, Janice Wiekamp, Viola Faber, Susan Klay, Verdell Kleinwolterink, Leonard Scholten.

Board of Directors—Northwestern State Bank
Front row, left to right: Robert M. Dunlop, Vice President; H. V. Rowenhorst, President; Elmer Huizenga, Vice President; Henry Te Paske, Attorney at Law.
Back row: Herman C. Moret, retired; William J. Cambier, Punt-Cambier Motor Company; Franklin Vogel, President of Vogel Paint and Wax Company, Inc.; Clifford Bogaard, President of Tri-State Livestock Auction Company; Earl T. Klay, Attorney at Law.

183

VOGEL PAINT & WAX CO. INC.

Present Modern Facility

Frank Vogel was born in 1865 at Friesland, Holland. At the age of 12 he became a painters helper and learned the trade of house painter, buggie and carriage painter or finisher.

In those days a good amount of the materials were made by hand grinding on the marble slab. Grandpa Vogel was an expert in woodgraining and was well respected in the painters trade. Today this is a lost art—antiquing came in its place.

Ten boys made up the family and most of the boys followed the trade some time of their life.

In the spring of 1913 the family immigrated to America and settled here, and in the year 1926 one of the ten boys, Andrew Vogel started what became the Vogel Paint & Wax Co. From a small beginning with two 18" steel burr grinders making only white house paint and red barn paint. Other items were added from week to week.

Andrew Vogel and his wife Jennie (Reinders) have five sons and two daughters. George, the oldest is located on the north side of the city park and operates a complete modern paint store. The other four boys, John, Frank, Arthur and Marvin operate the paint factory.

Claiming Orange City and its country side as their competitive trade territory, they soon capitalized on the motto, "Orange Brand paints cover Sioux County". In a few years "Orange Brand" paints were sold in Northwest Iowa and today it is sold throughout the Midwest, with some special items sold from coast to coast and in Canada.

A tour through the plant shows the visitor the modern ways of paint making.

Quality control is maintained at all times by the personnel and facilities of the testing laboratory.

A complete line of paint products for the building trade is manufactured both in oil and latex paints. Vogel's specialize in industrial finishes for the manufacturer of farm machinery and heavy equipment. Highway marking paints for states, counties and cities are made there by the truck loads. Daily production runs from four thousand to five thousand gallons. The paint is delivered daily by a fleet of company owned trucks.

With the main plant and office at Orange City they control the Vogel Paint Mfg. Co. at Omaha, Nebraska, the Nelson Paint Mfg. Co. at Sioux City, Iowa and the Diamond Paint Mfg. Co. at Marshalltown, Iowa.

This industry, which had its beginning before the turn of the century and is now entering the fourth generation of paint makers has played their part to make Orange City well known throughout the Midwest.

185

Andrew Vogel

Original Plant

Former Main Plant

Shows destruction the following day and the beginning of the clean-up. 247 loads were hauled to the dump. Many people of Orange City community came to help. Make shift areas were used to mix paint until the new plant was ready.

Shows people helping to carry out inportant records of paints.

Destructive Fire of June 3, 1964 shows firemen fighting blaze.

The Sioux Abstract Co., Inc., is also observing its 100th anniversary this year, having started the business of preparing abstracts of title to real estate in Sioux County, Iowa in 1870. The company was incorporated in 1919, and moved to its new office building, shown above, located across the street from the Sioux County Courthouse, in 1966 and is presently owned and managed by Wayland C. Breese and Albert J. Heemstra.

Predecessors in the business include W. H. Hospers, Jackson Hospers, O. N. Ross, F. J. Lohr, and C. W. Carter.

Prior names of the firm include M. E. Lewis & Co., Pierce & Lewis, Lewis & Dodge, Lenderink and Van Der Meide, and Van Der Meide & Lohr.

SIOUX ABSTRACT CO., INC.

The Evangel 4500

Evangel Aircraft Corporation is manufacturing, selling and servicing the Evangel 4500, a twin-engine aircraft designed particularily for operation in remote areas such as the Peruvian jungle, Canada, Alaska, etc. The Evangel 4500 is unique in that it provides the pilot with twin-engine reliability, short-field performance, ruggedness, reasonable cost and capabilities of carring a large bulky cargo.

The Evangel 4500 has been designed, developed and certified by a non-profit corporation called Evangel-Air, Inc. The development work was funded through contributions from God's people. The actual design and development began with and was directed by Carl Mortenson. Carl is a pilot-mechanic with the Jungle Aviation and Radio Service of Wycliffe Bible Translators. The ideas for the basic design were obtained while Carl was flying in Peru, South America with Wycliffe. A group of business men in Wheaton, Illinois organized Evangel-Air, Inc. to oversee the development of the aircraft which began in 1963 in Wheaton.

Evangel Aircraft Corporation was incorporated in 1965 to manufacture the Evangel 4500. The complete operation was transferred to Orange City in August, 1967 and the certification of the Evangel completed in early 1970.

EVANGEL AIRCRAFT

SILENT SIOUX CORPORATION

Silent Sioux Corporation was founded in 1921 by Mr. J. T. Grotenhuis, who is now chairman of the board. The major growth of the company to date was experienced under the direction of the late Mr. Dwight N. Grotenhouse, who was president from 1958 until his death in 1969. The elder Mr. Grotenhouse invented a noiseless oil burner which accounts for the company's name "Silent Sioux". Originally, the company produced oil burning space heaters in a small building downtown, but soon added a line of equipment for the poultry industry. Later the company moved into a building one block north of the present site. Shortly after World War II this building was destroyed by fire. The present building was completed in 1946.

BYLSMA BLACKSMITH SHOP

Mr. Peter Bylsma commenced business in Orange City in 1951 when he purchased the Blacksmith business from Case Van Ginkel, located at Third Street N. E. Previous ownerships by the late John Mulder and George Tolman only indicate the history of the Blacksmith business in Orange City.

In 1966 Mr. Bylsma purchased a portion of ground on the Southwest edge of the city, and there erected a new building of his own.

At this location he carries on, in the repair of farm machinery, tractors and many other items of smaller design.

Every consideration is given his customers and often times when the proper part is not available, Pete will create from forge and anvil a part which serves better than when newly manufactured.

RON'S DEEP ROCK

Ron Noteboom started in business for himself when in 1961 he purchased the Farm Delivery Gas and Oil business from his brother Peter.

In 1962 he purchased the service station from Don Van Ommeren. In 1965 he added the bottle gas business and in 1967 he expanded still a little further with a rental U-Haul dealership.

He now supplies two other service stations with gasoline.

He also operates a car wash in Hawarden, Iowa.

KORVER 5 & 10

This business was owned and operated for twnety-one years by James J. Korver. It was formerly a Ben Franklin Store, however, in 1967 he left the chain and became independent, thus the change in the name.

KLEM RADIO

KLEM Radio signed on the air in October of 1954, with 1000 watts of power at 1410 kilocycles. The studios and transmitter are located on highway 60, 2 miles north of LeMars.

Paul and Patti Olson purchased the station from George De Ruyter in July of 1961.

Since 1961, the staff has grown from 4 full-time to eleven full-time people with two part-time employees.

A strong news department is an important factor in the success of the station. Of the one-hour-forty-five-minutes of news given daily, 75% of it is of a local nature. Local meaning, primarily, Plymouth and Sioux County happenings.

Mercedes Moir, KLEM woman's program director, does a half-hour show daily. "Patterns for Living" is well received by thousands of KLEM-land housewives. The program offers homemaker features and special emphasis on community involvement.

In January of 1967, KLEM-FM became an addition to KLEM's total picture.

Located at 99.5 on the FM dial, with 47,500 watts of power, KLEM-FM, is operated as a separate station with fully automated equipment. Gene Van Grouw, of Orange City, is sales manager for the stations.

Powered by steam, this early trenching machine was used in Dallas in 1909.

100 years of progress . . . and, all of us at Iowa Public Service are pleased to join the citizens of Orange City in a salute to the traditions that have made this community such a wonderful place in which to work and live. IPS is proud that it has been privileged to do its part in supplying the comforts and convenience of natural gas 24 hours a day, every day. And, the folks of Orange City may further be assured that we will continue to offer low cost, dependable service.

IOWA PUBLIC SERVICE

These gas lights, including a gas reading lamp, were a 19th century luxury.

"ORANGE CITY NEWS MEDIA"

THE SIOUX COUNTY HERALD

The Sioux County Herald made its appearance in the year 1869 at Calliope, Sioux County, Iowa, but was moved to Orange City, before the county seat was moved from Calliope to Orange City. The earliest preserved issue was dated September 13, 1872, with L. B. Raymond as publisher. Earlier volumes and some later volumes are missing.

Mr. Raymond was succeeded by Henry and John Hospers. On November 21, 1873, J. J. Bell became the publisher, followed by C. W. Harmon on January 14, 1875.

On November 3, 1881, Mr. Harmon sold the paper to John Kolvoord and Harry P. Lewis. The firm Kolvoord and Lewis was dissolved December 21, 1882. Lewis carried on as publisher. On June 14, 1883, the masthead read: "Burke and Lewis Publishers", changing on April 10, 1884 to: "Harry Lewis and Co., Publishers."

The names of the publishers that followed are:
July 17, 1884, M. E. Lewis and Company
January 20, 1887, H. J. Lenderink
January 8, 1891, P. S. Junkin
October 19, 1898, George E. Bowers

No further particulars available. Mr. Bowers was the publisher of the last preserved issue dated December 25, 1907.

DE VOLKSVRIEND
June 18, 1874 — December 27, 1951

The dutch immigrants needed a newspaper in their native tongue to keep them abreast of the happenings of friends and relatives in scattered dutch settlements, as well as a medium for political discussions, and to report on church activities, marriages, births and deaths.

Of necessity this report in re De Volksvriend has to be brief.

Henry Hospers published the first issue of De Volksvriend (the people's friend) on June 18, 1874; a small Christian weekly with a subscription list of 120. In the year 1886 the size of the paper was enlarged to eight pages of the normal size. The number of subscribers grew rapidly; by 1922 the number had grown to more than 6,000.

The political affiliation of De Volksvriend was definitely Republican. Its rapid growth can be attributed to its wholesome contents, the large number of highly competent contributors and the faithfulness of seventy correspondents in twenty-five states.

The publishers of De Volksvriend were: Henry Hospers, John Hospers jr., Rev. K. Tietma, Antonie J. Betten jr., Dr. H. P. Oggel, John E. Oggel, H. P. Oggel & Son, J. H. Treneman, and for a few months, Percy R. Carney.

De Volksvriend's last issue was December, 1951.

THE SIOUX COUNTY LEADER

The first issue of the Sioux County Leader published in Orange City was dated September 17, 1885, Simeon D. McCumber, publisher. The publication appeared December 11, 1884 in Hawarden and had the name The Hawarden Leader.

With the issue of November 10, 1885, Lenderink and Vander Meide, real estate dealers, became the owners while McCumber continued in charge of the editorial department.

In the last issue on file, dated January 13, 1887, Vander Meide wrote that he was disposing of his interest in the Leader to H. J. Lenderink.

DE VRIJE HOLLANDER

This democratic newspaper in the Holland language was founded by M. P. Van Oosterhout in the fall of the year of 1902.

This weekly with some 2,000 subscribers blossomed soon into a bi-weekly. Herman Toering, associated with the paper some fifteen years, became the owner. The publication of the paper was suspended some time before Toering was appointed in 1919 to postmaster of the Orange City post office.

THE ORANGE CITY JOURNAL

No records existing, therefore no particulars available. The last owner and publisher was Joe Bailey.

THE SIOUX COUNTY CAPITAL

The first issue of the Sioux County Capital, a republican weekly, appeared December 19, 1935, James H. Treneman publisher and editor; Charles L. Dyke assistant editor.

Treneman sold the publication fifteen years later to Percy R. Carney. Less than a year later the paper changed ownership. The new owner, Fred Roach, published his first issue September 4, 1952.

In May, 1962, Fred Roach sold the paper to Wayne Stewart, who continues as publisher to the present date.

Tom J. De Jong started in real estate business in Orange City in partnership with Henry A. Jonker in January 1961. Henry A. Jonker passed away in December, 1961. He continued in the business as De Jong Real Estate. In May of 1964 he employed John B. Draayer as a salesman. In July of 1966 they entered into the partnership of De Jong and Draayer Real Estate. They have been at their present location since August 1966.

De Jong and Draayer Real Estate specialize in the sale of homes, farms, and business opportunities. They also make farm loans.

DE JONG AND DRAAYER REAL ESTATE

DUTCH MILL PHARMACY

The Dutch Mill Pharmacy is one of Orange City's newest establishments. This is a new business in a new modern building with modern ideas — all for the benefit of their customers. They carry a complete line of pharmaceutical, sundry and gift items.

The Dutch Mill Pharmacy is owned by Dwayne A. Plender, R. Ph., who was born and raised in Orange City; after receiving his education, he came back to serve his home folks.

HERITAGE HOUSE

Heritage House is a nursing home facility that provides total care for aging people. It is a completely modern facility, constructed in 1968 and has ample room for approximately 52 individuals. Included in the home are a spacious dinning room and lounging area. There is also a chapel where regular worship services are conducted by ministers and laymen of the area. Mr. and Mrs. Anthony Muilenburg are partners in the corporation and are the administrators of the facility.

DEPARTMENT OF AGRICULTURE

The Department of Agriculture in Sioux County was set up in 1933, through the Agriculture Adjustment Administration (AAA), better known as Triple A, with the first office located in the Court House. This was the beginning of the Commodity Loan Program and was administered by the elected County Committee. Peter E. Vermeer of Sioux Center was the first chairman. He was later succeeded by J. A. Armstrong of Hawarden.

In 1942, the Department shared the responsibility of food products during the war and in 1945 several agencies were consolidated into the Production and Marketing Administration (PMA), which consisted of the various Commodity Programs and the Agricultural Conservation Program administered by the Township and County Committees. Ed J. Armstrong as Chairman and served for many years.

In August of 1953, a change was made in the operation of the County Office and an Office Manager was appointed for the day to day operation of the County Office. C. A. Auchstetter of Hospers, who had served a short time as County Chairman, resigned to accept the position of County Office Manager and is now serving in that capacity. Jesse A. Yates of Hawarden was County Chairman for one year when John B. Draayer of Orange City was elected and has been the County Chairman since 1955. Other members of the Committee at the present time are Jake Abma of Rock Valley and Wendell Toentjes of Ireton.

The County Office is now known as the Agricultural Stabilization and Conservation Service (ASCS) and has successfully administered the Feed Grain Program since 1961, as well as the other Price Support and Conservation Programs.

The Department of Agriculture is both the product and creator of a century of change. It is now a cliche to say that Agriculture in Sioux County has changed more in a hundred years, than it had progressed world-wide in the previous twenty centuries. Change has come unevenly; with it problems. But Agricultural change has made possible the winning of wars and the building of a great industrial nation. Farmers and marketing men together have done such a good job, that Americans are able to feed their families with an average of only a fifth of their disposable income. This is far below most other countries.

County Committee — Left to right: Jake Abma, Vice-Chairman; John B. Draayer, Chairman; Charles A. Auchstetter, Office Manager; Wendell Toentjes.

NATIONAL FOOD STORES

National Food Stores have been a part of the Orange City Community for twenty-four years. During this time, they provided employment for hundreds of Orange City residents.

Many young people had their first job at the National Store. Being a nationwide company known for its good employees, many young folks used their National Foods experience as a springboard for many kinds of jobs throughout the nation.

National Food Stores promote an annual Scholarship program. The Sioux City Division of National Foods is well pleased with the number of winners produced by the areas served by the Sioux City Division.

Although there are National Food Stores from coast to coast, they operate as local businesses. Each area has its own warehouse that buys locally to supply its local stores.

The store managers are people who live in the towns they serve. They are people who are vitally interested in their communities and take an active part in its many projects.

PUNT – CAMBIER MOTOR COMPANY

John Cambier sr. left the farm in 1908 after his father died and became a partner of C. L. Dyk in the implement business on the corner where Cambier brothers erected the new building in 1912.

In 1910 Peter Cambier left the farm to go into partnership in the implement business with John Cambier. In 1912 John and Peter, the Cambier brothers, erected the large cement block building that was later occupied by Ed Utech and Edward Schreur.

From about 1914 to 1922 John Cambier was the ranking auctioneer of the area, and it was during this time that he held his famous implement sales. On a sale day as many people would come to town as for a Fourth of July celebration. One spring afternoon along with other implement sales, he sold an unbelievable eighty-five Racine corn planter.

In 1918 and 1919 the Cambier brothers erected the building which is now occupied by Punt-Cambier Motor Company.

In 1922 the partnership of Cambier brothers split with Peter Cambier retaining the implement business. John Cambier took in as a partner Wm. J. Cambier to open the Cambier Motor Company in the present building.

In 1932 both John and Peter Cambier died within a few weeks of each other. The implement business of Peter Cambier was sold to Ed Utech, and Wm. J. Cambier took over the management of Cambier Motor Company. For years Cambier Motor Company was the largest dealership in Northwest Iowa.

Old Livery Barn

1905 SIOUX VETERINARY CLINIC 1970

Sioux Veterinary Clinic of Orange City is proud to be the oldest continuously operated Veterinary Clinic in Sioux County.

In the early days of Orange City there were a few people of Dutch descent who administered to the health needs of horses and cattle. They were men who had received some training in Veterinary Surgery and medicine in Holland. These men practiced mainly on horses, treating the sick, injured, and lame as best they could.

Dr. Bradley Paxton was the first licensed graduate Veterinarian to come to Orange City. He was a graduate of Iowa State College, Ames, and in 1905 opened an office where the City Garage or Tolman's Alignment Shop is located today. He practiced here in this location until 1907. Not much is known of his work, but it could be assumed most of his practice would have been with horses.

Dr. H. J. Vande Waa, a 1906 graduate of Iowa State College, joined Dr. Paxton in practice in 1906. He was a son of Hendrick Vande Waa, one of the original four settlers of Orange City. Dr. Vande Waa maintained an office first in the city livery barn and then in the same building which became known as the City Garage.

In the year 1921, Dr. Vande Waa's brother-in-law, Dr. Edward Fisher, graduated from Iowa State College. Dr. Fisher joined Dr. Vande Waa in practice until Dr. Vande Waa's death in January of 1949.

It was in 1949 that Drs. Vande Waa and Fisher purchased the old blacksmith shop just east of the telephone office on Second Street. This was remodeled and became their new veterinary office. This was the same year the firm acquired another veterinarian. Dr. Robert Fisher moved to Orange City and joined the firm of Vande Waa and Fisher. Dr. Robert Fisher is the son of Dr. Edward Fisher. He was a 1940 graduate of Veterinary Medicine at Iowa State College in Ames. Since his graduation he had practiced at Ireton, Iowa, and in 1948 joined his uncle and father in practice at Orange City.

Old Blacksmith Shop

Sioux Veterinary Clinic

Sioux Veterinary Office

Upon Dr. Vande Waa's death in 1949, Dr. A. J. Neumann became associated with the veterinary firm. He was a 1949 graduate of Iowa State College of Veterinary Medicine.

Dr. Edward Fisher died in 1950 and the veterinary firm became Fisher and Neumann. It was in this year that the veterinary firm purchased and installed two-way radios, thus becoming the first radio-communication equipped veterinarians in Iowa.

In 1954, the firm purchased the old theater building on Second Street. On this site a new Veterinary Clinic building was constructed. It consisted of office space, drug room, small animal kennels and surgery room, and a large surgery room for large animals.

In January, 1959, Fisher and Neumann became known as Sioux Veterinary Clinic with the addition of two new partners, Dr. M. Vander Maaten, Sr., and his son, Dr. Martin J. Vander Maaten, Jr.

The old clinic was remodeled to accommodate four practitioners. A complete veterinary laboratory was installed and office accommodations were constructed. Drug room facilities were expanded and a new building constructed on east highway 10. This building contains a modern large animal operating room equipped with chute and operating table. There are a recovery ward, drug room, dog bathing room, office and kennels at this location.

Dr. M. Vander Maaten, Sr. graduated from Veterinary Medicine at Kansas State in 1929. He started practice in Alton, Iowa, in 1931 and moved in 1947 to Orange City.

His son, Martin J. Vander Maaten Jr., graduated from Iowa State College of Veterinary Medicine in 1956. He spent 1957 and 1958 in the Veterinary Corps of the United States Army. Upon his discharge from the army, he joined his father in practice in the latter part of 1958. Dr. Martin Vander Maaten Jr., left the Sioux Veterinary Clinic in 1960. He returned to Iowa State College to earn his doctors degree in Virology.

A heart attack in January of 1961 disabled Dr. Vander Maaten, Sr. He retired from active practice and Sioux Veterinary Clinic in December of 1961.

Drs. Fisher and Neumann continued to operate Sioux Veterinary Clinic until July of 1964. Dr. Robert Fisher retired from the practice to operate a motel at Buffalo, New York.

Dr. L. H. Royer, a 1962 graduate of Veterinary Medicine at Champaign, Illinois, joined the firm. He moved to Ireton in 1965 and manages the western end of the practice.

Sioux Veterinary Clinic today is the largest general practice in Iowa. We are proud of our service and veterinary facilities which are unsurpassed in Northwest Iowa.

Dr. Bradley Paxton—1905-1907

Dr. H. J. Vande Waa—1906-1949

Dr. Edward Fisher—1921-1950

Dr. Robert Fisher—1940-1950

Dr. A. J. Neumann—1949

STALLION

Dr. A. J. Neumann is the owner of eighteen of the finest registered Belgian horses in the United States. Among them are several well-matched teams. In the picture the doctor poses with "Jan Pieter Farceur", a three-year-old stallion that weighs twenty-two hundred pounds. (From the name one might conclude that "Jan Pieter Farceur" could have a little Dutch in his veins.)

Dr. M. J. Van Der Maaten Sr.
1959-1961

Dr. M. J. Van Der Maaten Jr.
1959-1960

Dr. L. H. Royer—1964-

Veterinarian Staff
Standing, left to right: Dr. A. J. Neumann; Dr. L. H. Royer; Dr. Kenneth W. Albrecht; Dr. David Christenson.
Seated: Mr. Edward Reinders; Mr. Albert Schuller; Mr. B. Zigtema.

201

E & J GIFT AND VARIETY

The E & J Gift and Variety Store started business in 1962. The name of E & J originated from the initials of the first names of the store owners, Mr. and Mrs. John Vermaat.

The Vermaat Family — Back row, left to right: Rebecca; Mrs. Vermaat; Mr. Vermaat; Arne. Front row: Bruce, Darwin.

LEMARS FEDERAL SAVINGS AND LOAN ASSOCIATION

The LeMars Federal Savings and Loan Association was founded, to promote thrift and home ownership, in 1934 at LeMars, Iowa. It was federally chartered at that time.

Mr. N. J. Bolser was secretary of the association and continued as such until his death in 1963.

From a minimal start it has grown to its present excellent financial status with assets of $14,099,-895.59.

It is interesting to note that in 1935 one year after its founding dividends amounted to ninety eight cents. In 1969 dividend payments figured at $580,490.99. The principal office is located at LeMars, Iowa. In 1969 they opened a branch office in a fine new building in Orange City, with Mr. Robert De Jong in charge.

"Meeting the needs of the community served has been and now is the goal of LeMars Federal Savings and Loan Association."

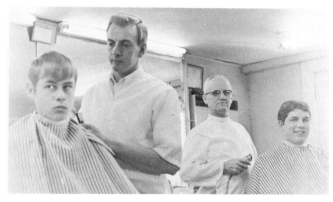

MODERN BARBER SHOP

Mr. John Van Bemmel came to Orange City in August, 1933, and rented the Barber Shop of Mr. Gerrit Popma located at 217 Central Avenue N. E. Mr. Popma stayed on as an assistant until 1936, when he retired after serving his community as a barber for fifty-one years.

In 1935 Mr. Van Bemmel moved his business to 113 Third St. N. W. where he remained until 1936 when he entered into a partnership with Mr. Jacob A. Oordt in a barber shop, located at 207 Central Avenue N. E. which they purchased from Mr. Cornie Van Surksum. After this partnership was dissolved in 1948, Mr. Van Bemmel managed the business alone until 1957 when he was joined by his son Harold, who continued until 1960.

From 1960 to 1962 Mr. Van Bemmel was assisted by his son-in-law, Mr. Don Pluim. In 1962 Mr. Pluim purchased a barber shop in Hull, Iowa and Harold Van Bemmel again joined his father's business, and remained until 1969 when he accepted a position with another business.

In 1962 Mr. Van Bemmel moved his business to the present location at 201½ Central Avenue, N. E. where Mr. Gerrit De Ruyter from Rock Valley, Iowa has assisted him since February, 1969.

Left to right: Lowell Van Zyl, Hospers, Iowa, Floyd Valley High School student; Gerrit De Ruyter; John Van Bemmel; Kelvin Korver, Dallas, Texas, student at Northwestern College.

The De Haan building as it appeared in horse and buggy days.

DE HAAN ELECTRIC COMPANY

The old red brick building with high, narrow windows and a decorated, stepped roof-line located on the corner across main street from the Windmill claims an age only thirteen years less than Orange City itself. Originally, it was the Orange City Bank Building, built by Henry Hospers in 1883. After the bank got caught in a panic and failed, the premises were vacant for a few years until 1917 when the United States Post Office moved there for thirty years.

P. J. Balkema then converted the structure into an appliance store until 1958, when Dr. D. Brink, a chiropractor, and Dr. A. Albertsen, an optometrist, established their offices there. In 1963 Franklin B. De Haan purchased the building and converted it into its present form as an appliance store.

The building just to the north is tied in closely with the corner structure. It was built by Henry Hospers in 1886 mainly to help support the narrow corner building, which the owner feared might topple over in a strong wind.

Originally it housed Geselschap's Drug Store. Sometime later Arend Hoff purchased the drug business and continued it until 1953. For the next six years John and Allen Roos used it for their electrical shop, and in 1959 Franklin B. De Haan converted it into its present use as an electrical and appliance store.

Left to right: Alfred Woudstra; James Woudstra; Lee Woudstra.

WOUDSTRA MEAT MARKET

The Woudstra Meat Market is perhaps one of the oldest continuous business places in Orange City. Meat markets have operated from this site almost from the beginning.

For many years John Synhorst measured out beef and pork at this location. Later it became known as Bouma's Market.

In 1926 James Woudstra purchased a one half interest from Sid Bouma and later acquired sole ownership.

The Woudstra Market has been largely a family type operation. Each of the Woudstra children has worked in the market at one time or another. In 1948 a new modern building was erected (note: on the very same site where meats had been handled for years). Equipment and fixtures were modern in keeping with the building structure. A frozen food locker system was included.

In 1955, the two sons, Al and Lee each purchased a third interest in the business. In 1967, Al and Lee took over their father's remaining holdings.

Their father James continues with a helping hand although his responsibilities have eased.

Today finds the third generation working behind the counters keeping the family tradition intact.

Dr. A. N. Albertsen was born in Humboldt County, Iowa. He attended school for Pre-Optometry training at the University of Nebraska, Lincoln. Optometry training was obtained at Northern Illinois College of Optometry, Chicago, Illinois.

He began the practice of Optometry in Orange City in March, 1958 at 107 Second St. N.E. which is known as the old post office building. In 1963 the practice was moved to a new building at 110 Second St. N.W. This building is on the site of the Korver Produce House, which was torn down when Bill Korver retired.

ALBERTSEN'S OPTOMETRY

LEGION BOWLING LANES

In 1955, the Legion Bowling Lanes building was constructed by Pressman Kosters Post 329.

The building was leased and the equipment was installed by Frank De Vries and opened for business on August first, 1955. Frank operated the business until September 30, 1961 at which time one half interest was sold to Ray A. Wielenga. Partnership was formed and operated as such until this time.

The bowling lanes and cafe has become one of the most popular meeting places for young and old in Orange City.

Van Gelder Jewelry was started as a business in Orange City, Iowa, on April 13, 1957. It began in the former Vande Waa Dry Cleaners and residence at 112 Second St. N. W. which is still its present location. It had its beginning in a small 12' X 19' space with a limited amount of merchandise and a repair department. However as the years passed it was enlarged and remodeled several times and now has approximately 1000 square feet of floor space to serve its customers with a complete line of diamonds, watches and jewelry items as well as a repair department. Mr. and Mrs. Dick W. Van Gelder own and operate the business.

VAN GELDER JEWELRY

KOHOUT CAP COMPANY

The Kohout Cap Company opened their new plant in Orange City in January of 1969. The new modern facility is built on a 10 acre site in the Orange City Industrial Air Park located just south of the city and adjacent to the municipal airport. The manufacturing plant and offices are in a 30,000 square foot building, single story, completely air-conditioned and equipped with the latest production equipment.

The company manufactures advertising caps and distribution is on a nationwide basis. Annual production is approximately 2,000,000 caps.

FARMERS MUTUAL COOP ASS'N

In 1908 a group of farmers recognized the need of facilities for the purchasing and marketing of their grain and supplies, met and organized the Farmers Mutual Cooperative Association. Products handled were grain, hogs, salt, twine, flour, feed and coal. Each member was sold one share at a cost of $25.00. Mr. Herman Tott, was hired as manager of this early cooperative. Sales the first year were $324,600.00. Within two years the company had 280 members. The company reorganized and reincorporated under a new code on November 16, 1936. During the following years many additions were made. A new office was built in 1946 and enlarged in 1963. Grain storage was built—steel quonsets and bins with a capacity of 182,400 bushels, a wood annex holding 30,000 bushels, and grain driers were also installed. In 1958 a fully modern feed manufacutring plant was built. A complete line of fertilizer equipment was installed for manufacturing mixed liquids, dry bulk fertilizer storage and blending, plus anhydrous ammonia equipment. In 1969 a concrete elevator was built at Orange City bringing total capacity there to 360,000 bushels. By 1970 the cooperative had nineteen regular employees, assets of nearly $1,000,000.00 and sales of approximately $3,000,000.00 annually.

New Elevator constructed in 1969.

WELLS BLUE BUNNY

Marion (Bud) Vander Laan and his Wells Blue Bunny milk delivery truck have been a familiar sight on the streets of Orange City for the past fourteen years. Bud provides delivery service, for the residential homes of Orange City with high quality grade A Blue Bunny dairy products. He also services the schools, rest homes, cafes, and the hospital. Other Blue Bunny trucks stop in Orange City to service the grocery stores with Wells milk and ice cream.

RUSSELL'S READY MIX, INC.

In 1951 Russell Vande Brake started an excavating business in Orange City. He also opened a ready-mix concrete business in Rock Valley, Iowa, that same year.

Expansion in 1954 saw the construction of a second ready-mix plant in Orange City.

The ready-mix concrete business seemed to hold great promise for the construction development urge of the future.

Plants were opened in Hartley, Sheldon, Paullina, Remsen, Alton, Marcus, and Ireton, Iowa bringing with it the requirement of larger facilities at the Orange City home plant.

Russell, now operating as Russell's Ready Mix, Inc., has extended into other areas of business. Presently, the firm at Orange City also manufactures pre-cast silos and feed bunks.

The industry from small beginnings has expanded to where it now has some fifty persons in its employ.

After several years of planning, Mr. Vande Brake entered upon another great enterprise in 1969. This year saw the completion of a new A. M. Radio Station KVDB with service to Northwest Iowa and adjoining states.

J & R BODY SHOP

On October 1, 1952 John R. Reinders and Marion Jasper joined in the partnership of J & R Body Shop. They opened for business at 112 First Street N. E., in the building now occupied by the ASC office. They offered a complete auto body repair business and front-end alignment service. In 1957 they moved to their present location at 110 Central Avenue S.W. On March 1, 1969 the partnership had to be dissolved due to the death of John R. Reinders and Marion Jasper became the sole owner. He continues its operation as an auto body shop.

Marion has had thirty years of experience in auto body repair and is well qualified to give complete and courteous service.

Left to right.

Roger Mouw; Herman Mouw; Lorenz Mouw

MOUW'S SUPER VALU

The Sanitary Meat Market was started in 1924 by William Kraai and Gerrit Bloemendaal. In 1926 Mr. Bloemendaal sold his interest to Mr. John Kraai In 1928 Mr. Herman Mouw began working for Kraai & Kraai and in 1934 became a partner in the in the business by purchasing Mr. Wm. Kraai's half interest in the meat market. With the purchase of Mr. John Kraai's interest in 1935, Mr. Mouw became the sole proprietor of the Sanitary Meat Market. Several years later Mr. Mouw's two sons, Lorenz and Roger began working in the market. The business was primarily a meat market until 1948 when a slaughter house, lockers and coolers were added to the establishment. In 1965 Lorenz purchased half interest in this business and in 1968 Roger bought Mr. Herman Mouw's remaining half interest in the business. Lorenz and Roger further expanded their business interests in Orange City with the establishment of a new super market which became operational on October 1, 1969 under the name of MOUW'S SUPER VALU where Lorenz is manager of the meat department and Roger is serving as manager of the grocery department.

FARMERS COOP OIL ASSOCIATION

The Farmers Union Co-operative Oil Association was organized as a Co-operative on May 24, 1935 by a group of energetic men who felt the need of a farmers organization in this territory. They named Frank Goergen president and John E. Jansen secretary.

After three years of business the union was resolved and on February 24, 1938 was incorporated under the name of the Farmers Co-operative Oil Ass'n. of Orange City, Iowa. The nature of the business was to conduct a general gas, oil and agricultural business.

Seven members were elected to be a board of directors, of which Joe Reinders was elected president and John E. Jansen secretary. Wm Schalekamp was named as manager.

From this beginning the organization has grown to do a $500,000 gross business. The current president and secretary are Henry B. Vander Zwaag and David Duistermars respectively. Wm Muilenburg is the present manager.

VILLAGE DRUG STORE

In 1919 a corporation was formed by the name of the Orange City Hotel Company. The founders were: Gerrit Klay, R. P. Dethmers, A. J. Kolyn, W. W. Schultz, J. J. Van Eizenga, Al Heemstra, Gerrit Bloemendaal, Steve De Jong and Peter Nissen. This corporation built the Hawkeye Hotel which was a landmark and a center of formal banquets, exquisite dining and a haven for travelers.

In 1944 the hotel was partially converted into a hospital by Dr. Wm. Doornink and became the medical center of Orange City until 1951. He continued practice in an office where the hotel lobby is now located until 1954. In 1955 Dr. D. Van Eldik reopened the office and practiced until 1957.

In 1953 Fred Van Sickle, owner of the Henry Lubbers Pharmacy then known as "Vans Drug", purchased the Hawkeye Hotel building which then housed the Charles De Vries "Gambles" Hardware Store, Hospital, Hotel and office space. Van Sickle converted the lobby and dining area into a drug store named the Village Drug and the office area was converted into the Village Cafe. Later Merlyn Kraai moved into the "Gambles" area and became known as the "Kraai Furniture Store". The hotel is presently managed by Mrs. Stella Houtsma and operates under the name of the Village Hotel.

In 1962 the Village Drug, Hotel and Cafe was purchased by Wayne Vernon and Richard Deets. Later that year, when Kraai furniture moved to its new location, the Village Drug was expanded and

remodeled and became known as the Village Drug, Inc. In 1968 the Village Cafe was closed and the "Tulip Town Gift House" became a new addition to the Orange City business community and is presently managed by Mrs. Bertha (Clarence) Peters.

PETER I. NOTEBOOM

Peter I. Noteboom began his business career in 1946 as the supplier of artificial ice in Orange City and surrounding towns of Alton and Sioux Center. The Noteboom name had long been familiar with the ice business as his father, Arie C. Noteboom had installed the artificial ice plant in Orange City about the year 1925.

Now he has one of the most unique businesses in the Orange City area, being the largest dealer of common live barn pigeons in the United States. An average of 100,000 pigeons pass through his pens each year at his farm located ¾ mile east of Orange City on highway 10. These are sold all over the United States and in some foreign countries. He also keeps a large drove of Appaloosa horses and one of only three buffalo herds in the state of Iowa.

Top row, left to right: Mark; Darryl. Seated: Mrs. Noteboom; Peter, Jr.; Peter I. Noteboom.

Paul Van Engelenhoven

Forrest D. Hubers

James D. Doornink

HUBERS - VAN ENGELENHOVEN - DOORNINK
INSURANCE AGENCY

The Hubers-Van Engelenhoven-Doornink Agency, Inc., is comprised of several agencies which served the Orange City area during the past fifty years. Records indicate that the original agency was the Synder Insurance Agency, which was purchased by William Westra in 1923. William Top entered the insurance business in 1929 when he purchased the William Westra Agency. Abe Schiebout started his own agency in 1940 and was joined by Paul Van Engelenhoven in 1962 and the agency was named the Schiebout - Van Engelenhoven Agency, Inc. In 1964 Abe Schiebout sold his interest in the agency to Forrest Hubers and the agency was named the Hubers - Van Engelenhoven Agency, Inc. William Top retired in 1967 and his agency became a part of the Hubers - Van Engelenhoven Agency,

Inc. In 1968 the Sipp La Fleur Agency was merged with the Hubers - Van Engelenhoven Agency. In 1969 the Doornink Insurance Agency merged with the Hubers - Van Engelenhoven Agency and the agency became known as the Hubers - Van Engelenhoven-Doornink Agency, Inc., The Doornink Agency dates back to 1929 when George Dunlop entered the insurance business. In 1946 Robert Dunlop joined his father in the agency. In 1958 Jack Int Veldt purchased this agency and sold it to James Doornink in 1966. With the heritage of the past agencies and agents, combined with the training and knowledge of the present agency members, the Hubers - Van Engelenhoven - Doornink Agency, Inc., is able to provide professional insurance services.

ORANGE CITY AD-VISOR

The original Ad-Visor was first published by the late Henry Noordhoff in 1936. For approximately ten years it was printed by mimeograph, in single 8½" x 14" sheets. In 1946 Mr. Noordhoff purchased an offset press and the Ad-Visor became the first offset paper in Orange City.

After publishing for 13 years Mr. Noordhoff sold his publication to Gerald Calsbeek, who published it for approximately one year and then ceased publication because of a new competitive free paper, known as the Merchant, which was established by John Post and Dick Van Gelder.

In 1954 The Merchant was bought by the local newspaper and that left Orange City without a shopping guide. When Harvey Pluim was discharged from the Air Force in 1955, he decided to start publishing the Ad-Visor again.

With a small loan to buy a used typewriter and an old offset press he printed the first issue in March, 1955. Because of a shortage of capital funds the publishing was done in the basement of his home at 314 4th Street, N.W. In 1957 the Pluim family moved to 121 Concord S.E. and the business again was operated from the basement. After publishing a small sheet for three years a new home was built at 412 Florida Ave. S.W. with accommodations for an office on the main floor and dark room and printing facilities in the basement. In 1962 a larger press was purchased and the Ad-Visor became a tabloid paper. After publishing a small tabloid for six years the printing was farmed out to be printed on a high speed roll fed press with a 32-page capacity at 10,000 papers per hour. The Ad-Visor is still published in this manner today, except that the format of the page has been changed to a full newspaper size.

In 1968 a building at 109 Central Ave. S.E. in downtown Orange City was purchased and completely remodeled. In July of 1968 the Ad-Visor moved into its present quarters where the shopping guide is published weekly along with a goodly amount of commercial printing. Several full and part time employees are employed by the Ad-Visor who are as follows: Keyron Schumacher, Fred Brandes Sr., Dennis Den Hartog, Dan Pluim, Linda Pluim, Mrs. Marlyn Bonnema, Mrs. Lloyd Van't Hof, plus eight carrier boys.

Mr. and Mrs. Harvey Pluim; Linda Kay, 17; Daniel Wade, 15; Lisa Jane, 11; Dale Harvey, 5.

The New Sales Pavilion

TRI-STATE LIVESTOCK AUCTION INC.

Mr. Clifford Bogaard commenced business as an auctioneer in 1948. In addition to crying farm and town sales, he worked as auctioneer in sale barns at Sheldon, LeMars, and Sioux Center, Iowa.

In 1956 he purchased a one half interest in the Auction Market at Sioux Center with Mr. Lou De Boer. This partnership continued until 1960 when, Mr. Ed Roetman purchased the De Boer interest.

In 1966 they erected new modern sales facilities one mile North of Sioux Center.

Tri-State Livestock Auction Inc. became the title at this new location indicating service to the three states of Iowa, Minnesota and South Dakota. Paul Den Herder was added as a third stockholder. Full and part time employees number thirty-six.

The firm is a member of the Certified Livestock Auction Markets Ass'n., fully bonded for customer protection and governed by the Brokers and Stock Yards Act.

Of interest for future generations are these re-

The three partners in the Tri-State Auction Company Inc. appear on the auction block. From left to right they are Edwin Roetman, Paul Den Herder and Clifford Bogaard. The auctioneers in the ring are Reynold Van Gelder at left and Dick Stene.

cords: during the year 1969 livestock sales figures reached $23,166,051.36. Livestock passing through the ring during this period are: cattle — 125,834; hogs — 80,991; and sheep 329.

The Old Sales Barn

A load of choice feeder cattle.

220

DE VRIES INTERIORS

Mrs. Cynthia De Vries opened a unique business in small capacity in February of 1953 — the manufacture of custom draperies. Mrs. De Vries, with one employee, Mrs. Grace Engbers, attended to the sewing while her husband, Mr. Steve De Vries, assumed the responsibilities of installation.

On June 10, 1965, Mr. Willis Rozeboom and Mr. Larry Baltzer purchased the De Vries interests, retaining the trade name of "De Vries Interiors." The building was doubled in size and completely modernized to the needs of their product.

Now, with increased personnel, they rank as one of the largest custom drapery and fabric centers in the Midwest.

AL'S FLOOR COVERING

In the early fifties Al De Haan purchased one half interest in the linoleum, counter top and wall tile business from Kraai Furniture.

In January of 1967 he acquired full interest in this business from Kraai Furniture and commenced business on his own at the corner of Central Avenue and Third Street N.E., where today their store is operated as a family affair.

Larry Kleinhesselink working with Al, takes full responsibility for all installation work. Mrs. De Haan assumes clerking and bookkeeping duties while their four children lend a helping hand on a part time basis. Their experience qualifies them not only for residential work but for all types of commercial and public buildings.

DYKEMA'S DEPARTMENT STORE

Dykema's Department Store opened for business in March, 1962, in the building which for many years had been the home of Vande Steeg's Store. It was remodeled and redecorated in modern well-lighted and air-conditioned fashion ideal for complete ladies wardrobe shopping.

They carry a complete line of women's and girls ready-to-wear clothing and shoes.

KALSBEEK BROTHERS

March 21 of the centennial year marks thirty years of Sales and Service to Sioux County and the Orange City area.

John and Art began business in 1940 with washer repairing and the sale of wringer type washers.

By the end of 1942 the brothers were involved in Uncle Sam's service.

Post war years, the business developed and included appliance sales.

1947 brought a new water supply into Orange City, which created a need for water conditioning, so Culligan Soft Water Service was added.

In the fifties, custom kitchen cabinets for remodeling were added.

The sixties called for more specialization so the appliance and bottled gas business was sold.

Now, the present location at 105 Third Street N. E. calls for full time Culligan water conditioning and custom kitchen planning.

DUTCH OVEN BAKERY

The Dutch Oven Bakery was established in the spring of 1954 by John Vermaat. He moved the equipment here from Ireton where he had previously owned a bakery. He and his wife, Everna, operated the business here until it was sold to Tony Huygens March 1, 1962.

For a time while John and Everna operated the bakery they had a whole-sale cookie and rusk business.

In 1957 Tony started working in the bakery and was employed there until he purchased it in 1962.

Tony came to the United States from Amersfoort, Netherlands in December, 1956. He was employed in Sioux City for a few months before coming to Orange City.

At present, Tony and his wife, Mildred, operate the business, which is two-thirds retail and one-third wholesale, with the help of thirteen full time and part time employees.

DE VRIES TRANSFER COMPANY

The De Vries Transfer Company was started in the year 1935 by Mr. Steve De Vries. Harold Paekel started working for him in 1943. He became a partner with Mr. De Vries and they worked together for ten years. Harold bought the entire business in 1962 and is the present owner. He continues to operate under the name of De Vries Transfer Company doing long distance moving.

Mr. and Mrs. Tony Huygens and daughter Kim.

KRAAI FURNITURE, LTD.

Kraai Furniture, Ltd. located on Central Avenue in downtown Orange City is one of the largest carpet and furniture businesses in the middle west.

Mr. Merlyn W. Kraai, president, currently employs twelve full time men consisting of salesmen, an interior decorator and arranger, four full time employees in carpet installation, a warehouse manager, and a delivery crew.

Mr. Kraai's thirty-five years experience in the carpet and furniture business began in 1935 when his father, William J. Kraai entered a furniture dealership. Mr. Kraai helped his father while attending high school and Northwestern Junior College in Orange City, and Morningside College in Sioux City. In 1942 William Kraai decided to pursue other business interests, marking the inception of Kraai Furniture under Merlyn Kraai. This business was started in the building presently occupied by the Fashion Shop. He continued business in this store until 1944 when he entered the U. S. Navy. In 1946 Mr. Kraai returned and began Kraai Furniture anew just two buildings south (presently bakery) of his first store. Since then, Kraai Furniture has steadily grown and expanded.

Merlyn Kraai

William Kraai

Cornelius Siebersma

In 1954 Mr. Kraai purchased another local furniture and hardware business and moved to a larger building across the street (presently Village Drug). The hardware business was discontinued within nine months. Since additional space and facilities were needed, Mr. Kraai in 1962 built his present display store east of Orange City's Windmill Square; shortly thereafter the large new annex and an additional new warehouse were constructed.

Sales activities are co-ordinated in the 6,500 square foot main Kraai Furniture Store and a 4,200 square foot furniture display annex. Furniture and carpet for installation are directed from the two display stores and two large carpet and furniture warehouses into a half dozen service and delivery vehicles which log hundreds of miles each day in Northwest Iowa.

In 1966 Cornelius Siebersma, jr., a former employee, renewed his association with Mr. Kraai. After Kraai Furniture's incorporation in 1968, Mr. Siebersma became a shareholder.

Kraai Furniture's desire to sustain customer confidence has augmented its business goal of maintaining a high volume of sales from a large inventory of quality carpet and furniture.

GROEN PLUMBING AND HEATING
AND AIR CONDITIONING

The firm was founded in 1929 by John Groen. Later his son Calvin joined with him in this business and today Calvin is the sole owner of the firm. During the firm's forty-one years in business, most noticeable is the change in the customer demands and needs. The change from the manual operated coal and wood furnace to completely automatic systems and including air conditioning, from windmills to force pumps and electrical pressure systems. A complete change in the sheet metal and tin work as compared to forty years ago. Also noted is that in the earlier years of the firm all ditches for sewer and water lines were dug by hand. Today jeep trenching and back-hoe digging speeds up this tedious task. Even the humble job of cleaning sewers is done with electrical equipment. Looking into the future the firm wonders what the next century will bring.

L & K CLOTHING

In February of 1957 Wally Luhrs and Orrie Koehlmoos from Paullina, Iowa were on their way back from Hull, Iowa where they were planning to start a men's and boys clothing store. On their return trip they traveled by way of Orange City where they talked to Leon Roggen and Fred Van Sickle. Leon and Van convinced them they should start the clothing store in Orange City. With the help of Van Sickle they secured a lease on the Corner Cafe building located at the corner of First and Central from Minnie and Albert Grooters.

The building was remodeled and new fixtures installed, and on April 6, 1957 they opened for business, carrying a complete line of men's and boys clothing and men's shoes. Luhrs managed and operated the clothing store while Koehlmoos traveled as salesman for the H. D. Lee Company.

Enlarging the corner building as much as possible, and with the clothing and shoe business continuing to grow, Luhrs and Koehlmoos decided they needed more space. April 1965 they purchased the Eerkes building, located at 107 Central Avenue where L & K is now located. With additional space they were able to increase their clothing and shoe departments and added a sporting goods department.

L & K has expanded to several partnership stores in Iowa, located in Pella, Grinnell, Clarinda and Hamburg.

SIOUX ELECTRIC COOPERATIVE ASSOCIATION

Sioux County is the land of pioneers. The sturdy folk who traveled by covered wagon to this area more than one hundred years ago stayed to build their homes and raise their families on the rich, prairie soil. The fine, black farmland produced good crops, and the farmers prospered.

But, in 1936, most of the farm people of Sioux County were living under conditions not too much improved over pioneer days. Lacking electricity, these farm people had no opportunity to light their homes properly. Water had to be pumped or carried by hand for household purposes as well as farm chores. Lanterns were the general mode of lighting about the farmyard, sometimes with disasterous results.

An old-fashioned washboard was an important item in every farm wife's home, unless she was fortunate enough to have a washing machine powered by a gasoline engine and a willing husband to stand by to help operate it! Electric refrigeration was found in the city shops, or in the homes of fortunate town friends.

Shortly after president Franklin Roosevelt signed the Rural Electrification Act of 1936, the pioneer-spirited Sioux County farm people began preliminary work to bring central station electric service to their farms. Guided by Farm Bureau leaders, H. S. Nichol and Ken Wagner, the Sioux County region made a united effort to secure loan funds from the Rural Electrification Administration (REA), and on July 18, 1938, the Sioux Electric Cooperative Association received its charter from the State of Iowa.

But, those were the days of the depression, and in many cases, it was difficult to convince farm neighbors that rural electrification could become a reality through a cooperative. Moreover, many of the farmers did not have the $5.00 required for the membership fee, nor were they certain they could use and pay the minimum of $3.50 per month which was also a requirement.

With a persistence born of need and determination, the early organizers eventually secured enough members to make it feasible to request a government loan. In October, 1938, the REA approved the initial loan to the Sioux Electric Cooperative Association.

Soon a contract for construction of the first lines was let; construction of the highline was an actuality. The first substation was energized on July 1, 1939, and the first members received service shortly thereafter.

One of the first employees of the new organization was Eugene C. Mulder, who was employed in the fall of 1938 as easement solicitor and project coordinator. In July, 1939, he was appointed system manager, a position he retains to this day.

Initially the association shared offices with the Sioux County Farm Bureau in the basement of the courthouse. Then in early 1939 office space was leased in the Dyke building on the east side of the City Park. A quonset hut in the south part of town served as a warehouse and vehicle garage. In 1951 negotiations were begun to purchase property along highway 10 east of Northwestern College for the purpose of constructing the modern office building and warehouse which was finally completed in early 1956. In 1961 a much-needed garage-warehouse addition was constructed, and a further enlargement was completed in 1966. The present building has ample space for offices, garage storage, and warehousing.

After the first highlines were constructed and the first member-consumers received electric service, more farmers were eager to have the benefits of electric power on their farms. At the end of the calendar year 1939, the Cooperative was serving 435 member-consumers, on approximately 200 miles of line. At the close of 1969, there were 2,080 member-consumers with 915 miles of line. The first substation, known as the Orange City substation, had a capacity of 300 KVA. Today, that much capacity may be required for one commercial member-consumer. At the present time the Cooperative is served by five substations with a total capacity of 11,000 KVA, and early in 1970 a sixth substation will come into service in the Sioux County area.

Sioux Electric Cooperative Association Office Building and Warehouse on Highway 10.

When the first REC lines were energized, the main usage of electricity was for lights, possibly a washing machine and electric iron, a radio and perhaps a milking machine. During the year 1939 member farmers used a monthly average of 49.7 KWH's. During 1969 the average was no less than 1,280 KWH's per meter per month. Electric power is being widely used for heating systems, crop drying, silo unloading, and automatic feeding, and the modern farm wife often has more electrical conveniences and aids than her city counterpart.

Another pioneering effort of the Sioux Electric Cooperative was its membership in the Northwest Iowa Power Cooperative to bring low-cost electric power to northwest Iowa. Through the combined efforts of the ten member cooperatives, electric power was brought to the area from the Bureau of Reclamation dams on the Missouri River.

When it became evident that "Bureau" power would not be adequate power, the Sioux Electric Cooperative joined with other cooperatives in organizing Basin Electric Power Cooperative at Bismarck, North Dakota. At the present time member-consumers of the Sioux Electric are receiving electric power from the series of hydro-electric dams on the Missouri River as well as the lignite coal plant in Bismarck operated by Basin Electric Power Cooperative.

Two Orange Cityans serve on the present board of directors. Gillis Haverdink is president and Harold E. Vermeer is vice president. Including manager Eugene C. Mulder, the present employees number eighteen, conducting the various departments of service for the member-consumers. The maintenance and operations department is headed by Alfred L. Bomgaars, line superintendent, with Bud Van Otterloo, Francis F. Streff, Clarence E. Postma, Otto A. Huizenga, Paul M. Winchell, and Gerald D. Fedders as linemen. The service department which handles electrical wiring services of all kinds for REC members is supervised by George Kleinhesselink, with Corneluis Eshuis and Donald Bruxvoort as assistants. Gerald S. Calsbeek is in charge of electric meters and electric heating installations. Cecil F. Keith is in charge of all material, hardware receipts and disbursements, and also is building and grounds custodian. The office force consists of office manager Mildred Hansen, Mary Ann Winchell, Sharon Goering, Evelyn Moss, and Gerrit G. Kroeze.

Fourteen of the employees are permanent residents of Orange City, and thirteen are home-owners here. All are active in community and church affairs and interested in doing their best for the members they serve and the neighbors among whom they live.

The Sioux Electric Cooperative Association came into being through the united efforts of a dedicated group of pioneering farmers in Sioux County who sought an answer through cooperation to their needs for rural electric service. Today the Cooperative has grown through the continued efforts of its member-consumers and continues to pioneer in securing needed low-cost power for the Sioux County area.

NORTHWEST IMPLEMENT COMPANY

Northwest Implement Company is located on Highway 10 West and is owned by James L. Wassenaar and Wm. De Koter.

It was formerly located at third street and operated by Mr. Andrew Oordt under the name of Oordt Implement. Mr. James L. Wassenaar became a partner in the business in 1963. The following year Mr. Oordt retired, and Mr. William De Koter, who had previously owned the De Koter Repair Shop at Maurice, Iowa, purchased a share in the business.

Northwest Implement Company offers a complete line of International Harvester machinery and trucks, as well as New Idea, Kewanee, Westendorf, and Broyhill. They also have a service department to service all brands of machinery and truck.

POPMA RADIO AND TELEVISION

Entering into business in 1930, Frank Popma is now ready to embark upon the fifth decade of his business. His area is in the ever-changing world of radio, television and electronics.

In the mid-twenties Frank became interested in radio repair. Schooled in its complications he opened shop as a branch of the De Jong Furniture, in the Hawkeye Hotel building, (now Village Drug).

These were the good old BATTERY radio days, few tubes, many dials, earphones and much static. These were the interesting days of 8¢ bread, 5¢ milk, 4¢ pork, 6¢ beef, and 9¢ gasoline. A Popma service call 75¢. It took three months of labor and two acres of land to buy what was then a good quality radio.

Then came the forties with its wars, rural electricification and many other discoveries.

The fifties followed with television bringing sports, music and drama into the living room.

The inflated sixties—more knowledge in all fields, especially electronics, producing transistor radios, modules, print boards, F. M., remote control, and color television. The dollar bill became a shrunken rag but it took only one acre of land to buy, not a battery radio but the finest in color television.

With the seventies at hand the field of electricity holds out greater promise and possibility of advancement than in any earlier decade.

AUTO SERVICE GARAGE

During the early days, when the automobile was replacing "OLD DOBBIN" in the realm of transportation, Mr. Henry Den Hartog Sr. took the initiative to erect a building, in what was then the extreme Southwest part of Orange City. (Developments have extended considerably beyond this point now). The year was 1921.

His five sons, Henry Jr., James, Cornie, John and William here opened an automobile and truck repair business—each dedicating himself to become thoroughly familiar in some specific phase of motor repair.

They operated under the trade name of "Den Hartog Bros. Garage" and soon gained the reputation that if an automobile can be repaired, "Den Hartog Bros. can Fix It!"

As time went on, the next generation (grandsons of Den Hartog Sr.) were added to the employee personnel. Changes were made in the building structure and modern equipment was added to cope with the everchanging design of the motor industry.

One of the grandsons, Clarence Den Hartog, in 1952 started business for himself in the Utech Building under the trade name of "Auto Service Garage". In the meantime Grandpa, Henry Jr. and James passed on. In 1962, when Cornie, John and William retired, Clarence purchased the building and now continues in business at the location where his forebears had their beginning. He retained the title of the business as, "Auto Service Garage."

With his 25 years of experience the reputation of, "WE CAN FIX IT" has been maintained.

HI – PRECISION

Hi-Precision Manufacturing Company has completed its twenty-second year in business in Orange City.

Mr. Albert S. Hancock, jr., president, came to Orange City in 1947, and was employed by Silent Sioux Corporation as chief engineer. While there he began the bullet business as a sideline, but as the business grew it became necessary to devote full time to it.

In 1952 they began manufacturing three-bladed arrowheads in addition to the bullet line, and now supply every major archery equipment manufacturer in the United States.

They presently manufacture more than one hundred different copper-jacketed bullets (projectiles only) which range from 17 caliber to 50 caliber.

The factory has been running twenty-four hours a day since October, 1957.

Bullets

Dr. E. B. Grossmann, Jr.
Surgeon

DR. E. B. GROSSMANN, Jr.

In November 1969 Dr. E. B. Grossmann, Jr. joined the Orange City medical community as its first fully trained general surgeon. He presently has his office at 111 Central Ave. S.E. and is serving as general surgeon in Orange City and surrounding communities.

Office at 111 Central Avenue S.E.

Office at 322 Albany Avenue S.E.

PETER PALS — DDS

The dental office constructed in 1958 by Dr. L. K. Meier was sold to Dr. Peter W. Pals in October, 1968 who at that time began his practice of general dentistry in Orange City.

Dr. Pals had two years of his undergraduate education at Calvin College, Grand Rapids, Michigan, followed by one year of undergraduate study at the State University of Iowa, Iowa City, Iowa. He entered the college of Denistry at the State University of Iowa in 1961 and received his degree of Doctor of Dental Surgery in 1965. Following this, he served an internship at Martin Army Hospital, Fort Benning, Georgia. He completed military service in May, 1968 and practiced as associate in Forest City, Iowa before moving to Orange City.

Former Repair Shop on Albany Avenue.

TOLMAN WELDING AND MANUFACTURING

The Tolman Welding and Manufacturing Company was started in the spring of 1946 on an acreage near Alton, Iowa, using a cob shed as their first shop. In the fall of 1946 construction was started on a building on South Albany Avenue which was used as a repair shop. In 1954 the facilities were expanded to nearly double its original size due to the increase in repair business; also to accomodate the new business of fabricating structural equipment for ready mix and fertilizer plants. This building is now leased to Otis Radio and Electric Company.

During the year 1962 five and a half acres of land were purchased a mile and a half East of Orange City on highway 10.

A large new building with ample facilities was constructed and occupied in 1963. The services then were expanded to custom manufacturing, building material, handling equipment for the fertilizer industry, grain, packing plants and rendering companies.

In 1969 the old City Garage was purchased and converted into an auto alignment and safety check business. This business is now operated by Alan Tolman, son of William Tolman.

Modern Manufacturing Plant on Highway 10.

Al's Alinement Service on 117 Central Avenue S.E.

Office of Kepp Construction on Highway 10.

KEPP CONSTRUCTION COMPANY

Kepp Construction Company was established by W. A. Kepp in 1908 at Rochester, Minnesota and operated in that area for a number of years.

For approximately twenty years the firm was located at Rapid City, South Dakota, and then worked East again in the middle thirties and relocated at Rochester, Minnesota. From this location the company built power plants in a five state area until moving to Orange City, Iowa in the spring of 1947.

The change in location was made since for a period of ten years most of the work under contract had been in Iowa. In the spring of 1947 the firm had two power plants in Eastern Nebraska,

three in Iowa and one in Southern Minnesota. Orange City was centrally located for this work.

The firms first job in Orange City was the Municipal Power Plant. Since locating in Orange City the firm has constructed locally seven buildings for Northwestern College, the Municipal Hospital, Medical Clinic, sewage treatment plant, old high school, Northwestern State Bank, LeMars Federal Savings & Loan, American Reformed Church, Sioux Electric Coop, Unity Christian High School and numerous commercial buildings.

The firm has operated within an eighty mile radius of Orange City since about 1949, confining itself to schools, churches, and public buildings.

Office at 104 Central Avenue N.W.

Donald Vander Weide

NEW YORK LIFE INSURANCE COMPANY

The New York Life Insurance Company has been represented in Orange City since 1925, by Walter Aardappel, Arie Vander Stoep, and Don Van Der Weide.

In the early years of New York Life's representation in this area, an average size policy was approximately $2,500.

The insurance purchased by New York Life's policyholders through this local office has been thirty million during the past ten years.

ORANGE MOTOR COMPANY
OLDSMOBILE DEALER

Orange Motor Company was established in 1954 by John Harvey De Vries, in the frame building now occupied by the Wooden Shoe Factory on Fourth Street S. W. Later the business was moved across the street to the north.

In 1954 Mr. Orville De Jong purchased the dealership from De Vries. In 1967 Mr. De Jong purchased the Slagle Lumber Company property at the corner of Arizona and Third Street S. W., erecting a new building. The sales agency and the service garage are now being conducted at this location.

In 1959 Jay De Jong joined his father to take over the sales responsibilities.

Windmill Park Apartments—3rd Street and Arizona

The Donald Mouw residence, 302 Florida Avenue N.W.

DON MOUW CONSTRUCTION CO.

The Don Mouw Construction Company, who specialize in building quality homes and condominium's in and around Orange City since 1957, also do general construction work. At present the company employ five men. They are: Martin De Wit, Jerry Goedhart, Gary Cleveringa, Ben Vander Zwaag, and Marlin Wielenga. Mr. Albert Van Leeuwen of Hospers has been working part time since his retirement.

Don was born and raised on a farm Northeast of Orange City. His grandfather, Maas Mouw was an early settler in this area and a member of the First Reformed Church at Orange City.

Mr. and Mrs. Mouw are members of Trinity Reformed Church and parents of two daughters, Kathleen 16 and Laurel 11. Mrs. Mouw is secretary-bookkeeper for her husband's business.

THE DUTCH MILL INN

The Dutch Mill Inn opened its doors in May of 1969. Incorporation papers were filed in July of 1969 with Frank Vogel and Cliff Bogaard as incorporators.

The restaurant, done in Dutch decor, offers a seating capacity in its coffee shop and dining room of 125. An additional meeting and party room is available in the lower level seating approximately eighty-five. A special feature of the dining room is the many reproductions of Rembrandt paintings.

A complete breakfast - luncheon - dinner menu is offered at the Dutch Mill Inn.

In 1969, Mr. Dan Becker became a partner in the corporation and is manager of the restaurant.

From left to right: Mrs. Bogaard; Clifford Bogaard; Daniel Becker; Franklin Vogel; Mrs. Vogel.

George Dunlop

Mrs. George Dunlop

Mr. and Mrs. George Dunlop

Mr. and Mrs. George Dunlop settled in the Orange City community in January, 1916. Mr. Dunlop, proud of his Scotch ancestry, was County Extension Agent in this area and soon became active in church, civic, farm, and school activities. In his farm work he served as president of the Sioux County Fair for twenty-five years, and distributed farm supplies through his Dunlop Insurance Agency. He was president of the Chamber of Commerce and the local Lion's Club, as well as a volunteer fireman for twenty years. George was vitally interested in the local school and was a member of the school board for twelve years, serving as its president for nine of those years. Perhaps his great-est satisfaction was to be found in his civic efforts as chairman of the fund-raising campaign for the Orange City Municipal Hospital. He was also an ardent worker for the annual Tulip Festival and served as general chairman of this event for twelve years. His church work included participating as a teacher, Sunday School superintendent, and as an elder in the American Reformed Chruch. His wife, Florence, also served the community, participating untiringly in the Tulip Festival, the local Woman's Club, and many church activities. Mr. and Mrs. Dunlop raised three children in Orange City—a daughter, Maragret Jean, and two sons, Robert Mitchell and Donald Dean.

5oth Wedding Anniversary Celebration of Mr. amd Mrs. Pieter D. Van Oosterhout at the home of Mr. and Mrs. William H. Van Oosterhout, Wilmette, Illinois, May 30th, 1948.
Seated, left to right: Marie and Kenneth Pollard; Pieter, Wm. H., and Sarah Van Oosterhout; Richard, Burchard, Cornelia (Neale) and Susan Ashenfelter.
Standing: Donald Pollard, Charles Pollard; Martin, Ethel and Peter Peter Van Oosterhout; Edna, Sarah, Wm. H. and Mary Van Oosterhout.

VAN OOSTERHOUT

Pieter Van Oosterhout (1790-1876) of Te's Grev-elduin-Capelle, Nort Brobant, Nederland, and his wife Dingema (April 26, 1810 - October 16, 1889) had one child, Martin Pieter (October 14, 1846 - October 12, 1906). In disagreement with his country's South African policy, Martin sold all his property and with his mother, wife, Cornelia Wilhelmina de Bruijn (April 26, 1852 - October 16, 1935), and four children emigrated to Pella, Iowa. After two and one-half years at Pella, Iowa, and one year at Holland, Michigan, they came to Orange City.

Vitally interested in politics and events–local, national, and European–he returned to the Netherlands several times and was influential in raising money for Christian National Instruction in South Africa. He served on local independent school boards and supported Christian education.

Warned of impending death from diabetes unless he would strictly diet, he refused to diet and made preparations for his death on October 12, 1906. These preparations included the erection of a family mausoleum in the local cemetery.

The Van Oosterhout children were: Dingena Cornelia Jacomina Adriana who never married; Geertruida Dingena Catharine who married Rev. Nicholas Burggraaf; Dirk Adriaan Antonie who married Jennie Brolsma, and Pieter Dirk who married Sarah Anna Hospers, the daughter of Wm. Hospers.

Pieter Dirk was a graduate of Liberal Arts and Law Colleges of the University of Iowa, Columbia Graduate College of Law, and Phi Beta Kappa. He was a "half-back" on the University football teams in 1892 and 1893 and the editor of the student newspaper, the Vidette (later "Daily Iowan"). He entered law practice in Orange City in 1894 and served on the school board, as Mayor, and as Sioux

Three Generations — Left to right: Martin Pieter Van Oosterhout, Martin Donald Van Oosterhout, Pieter Dirk Van Oosterhout. Picture taken 1904.

Three generations — Left to right: Hon. M. D. Van Osoterhout, Peter D. Van Oosterhout, Pieter Dirk Van Oosterhout.

County Attorney. A happy day for him was when he returned in June of 1953 to see his oldest grandchild, Peter Denne, receive a B.A. degree from the University, also a Phi Beta Kappa, just sixty years to the week since he had received a like degree.

Mr. and Mrs. Pieter Dirk Van Oosterhout are survived by four children—Martin Donald; Mrs. L. Pollard (Marie Cornelia) of Toledo, Ohio; William Hutchinson, a Chicago lawyer from Wilmette, Illinois; Mrs. Burchard Ashenfelter (Cornelia Marie) of South Bend, Indiana; eight grandchildren and seventeen great-grandchildren.

Martin Donald is the only fourth-generation Van Oosterhout to remain in Orange City. He entered the law firm of his father in 1924. He is a member of the Order of the Coif, honorary law degree of the American Law Institute, served as Sioux Coun-

ty Representative in the Iowa Legislative Sessions for two terms, and as Chairman of the Interim Committee. In 1943 he was elected Judge in the Iowa 21st Judicial District, and in 1955 was appointed by President Eisenhower to the U.S. Eighth Circuit Court of Appeals where he is now Chief Judge. He is married to Ethel Greenway, a graduate of Capital City Commercial College, Des Moines, Iowa, and Iowa State University, and former Sioux County Home Demonstration Agent. Their only child, Peter Denne, graduated from local public schools and Liberal Arts and Law Colleges of the University of Iowa, served as an officer in the Air Force for two years, and is now president of Growth International Inc. He resides in Cleveland, Ohio, with his wife and three children, Sarah, Susan, and Peter Dirk.

**THESE CITIZENS BECAME NINETY YEARS OF
AGE OR MORE IN 1970.**

Mr. Sikke Hoogeterp

Mrs. John Behrend

Mr. Martin Van Peursem

Mrs. Henry Haarsma

103 Great Grandchildren   7 Great-Great Grandchildren

Mr. Otto Mouw; Mr. John Postma; Mr. James Schuller

Mrs. Tjerk De Vries

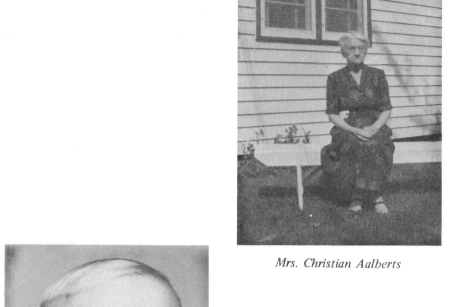

Mr. Evert Reinders

Mrs. Christian Aalberts

Mrs. Henry Van Leeuwen

Mrs. Jake Van Marel

Mr. and Mrs. John Buurman

Mr. and Mrs. Tony De Haas

Mr. and Mrs. Ben Vande Griend

Mr. and Mrs. Gerrit Huitink

Mr. and Mrs. Gerrit Top

Mrs. Koenraad De Jong

Koenraad De Jong

Koenraad De Jong was a son of Koenraad De Jong Sr. who emigrated with his five children from Holland to Pella, Iowa in 1847. He was united in marriage to Petronella Van Zee in 1871.

He was the first of the De Jong brothers to settle in Sioux County. He was a successful farmer for a number of years after which he moved to Orange City and gave the rest of his life to public service.

Mrs. Charles Sterrenburg of Orange City is the only living member of the Koenraad De Jong family.

Nelson De Jong and old corn stalks

98 YEAR OLD CORN STOCKS

Mr. and Mrs. Gerrit De Jong and family came from Pella, Iowa in 1870 and claimed a homestead 3 miles south and 3 miles west of the Northwestern College corner. In 1872 Mr. De Jong built a barn and learned that he lacked lumber to complete the project. Having an innovative bend of mind he improvised by cutting corn stocks (from the first corn crop on his farm) and tied them into bundles with bands made of prairie hay. He placed the bundles under the eaves and on the hay-loft to insulate the structure. In 1914 Gerrit's son, Peter G. De Jong, razed the barn and preserved a bundle of the corn stocks that are displayed in the picture by Nelson De Jong a grandson of Gerrit. The farm is still in the De Jong family. Harry De Jong, also a grandson of Gerrit, owns the land and his son, Paul De Jong, farms it.

Back row, left to right: Henry, John, James, Andrew, Howard.
Front row, left to right: Albert, Hilbert, Grandpa, Gus, Grandma, Frank, Dick.

Mr. and Mrs. Andrew Vogel

The Feike Vogel Family

In the month of March, 1913, the Feike and Grietje Vogel family immigrated from Berlikum, Netherlands, to the United States, arriving in Grand Rapids, Michigan. They had ten boys, the three oldest, Albert, Henry, and John, already had made the trip one or two years before.

The following year, 1914, they moved as a family to Orange City, Iowa, and in 1916 they moved to a large farm near Bigelow, Minnesota. In the Netherlands they were a family of painters and all the older boys followed this trade, except John who was a baker.

At one time they had a family orchestra of seven pieces. Albert played the organ and Henry for a time was band director and song leader.

Andrew is the only one of the Vogel Brothers that remained in Orange City. On December 26, 1919 he was united in marriage with Jennie Rein-ders, daughter of Mr. and Mrs. John R. Reinders. They have seven children whose names are as follows: Franklin, George, John, Arthur, Marvin and Margaret (Mrs. Roger Roghair) all of Orange City and Bertha (Mrs. Maynard Stephenson) of Sioux City, Iowa.

Mr. Vogel, being a member of a family of painters, began his painting and decorating business at an early age. He soon began mixing his own paints and in later years, with the help of his sons, developed the business into one of the largest paint manufacturing and distributing operations in the middle west known as the "Vogel Paint and Wax Company."

The Vogels have contributed substantially to the development of Orange City. Moreover, they are active in community projects and are loyal supporters of the christian church.

The picture of Mr. and Mrs. Andrew Vogel was taken for their fiftieth wedding anniversary which was on December 26, 1969.

Hubert Muilenburg

Hubert Muilenburg is remembered and honored as one of the founders of the Orange City community. He was born in Holland in 1822, seven years after his father helped stop Napolean in the Battle of Waterloo.

Not satisfied with his native land, he and his wife, and three-year-old daughter spent fifty-two days on a sailing ship to come to America in 1848. Working up the Mississippi River from New Orleans, the family witnessed the horror of a slave auction and survived a dreadful cholera epidemic before they finally trudged into Pella, Iowa, by ox team in 1851. Mr. Muilenburg was one of the four men who made the first exploration for the Holland settlement in Northwest Iowa.

Hubert Muilenburg's son, Samuel, was ten years old when the family moved from Pella to Orange City. After marrying Adrianna Marie Markus, Samuel Muilenburg purchased a bare prairie farm ten miles west of Orange City in 1886.

Active in the development of Orange City, Samuel Muilenburg presided at the organizational meeting of the Farmers Cooperative Elevator. He was a charter consistory member of the Farmers Cooperative Elevator. He was a charter consistory member of the Trinity Reformed Chruch, and he served as first president of the Pioneer Memorial Home from 1927 until 1942, only thirteen years before his death in 1955 at the age of 93 years.

Mr. and Mrs. Samuel Muilenburg
(This picture was taken at the Muilenburg home in 1920 during the 50th Anniversary of Orange City.)

Mr. and Mrs. Henry K. Bekman

Born in the Netherlands in 1875, Henry K. Bekman sailed for America with his parents and his grandparents in the spring of 1899.

That summer the elder Bekmans settled in Alton, but by fall Henry Bekman had married Anna Muyskens, also born in the Netherlands, and had moved to Orange City to found a tailor shop which he owned and operated until his death on Christmas Day, 1915.

John T. Klein family — Mr. and Mrs. Klein; children, left to right: Tunis (deceased); Kittie (Mrs. H. J. Vande Waa); Gertrude (Mrs. Edward Fisher).

Gerrit Van Horssen family — 1889 — Left to right: Mrs. Van Horssen; Anna (Mrs. H. Brink); Lizzie (Mrs. H. K. De Jong); William Van Horssen.

The William Reickhoff Family — Mr. and Mrs. Reickhoff and children, Robert, Phyllis (Mrs. Sam Lincoln) and Lawrence.

The late William H. and Marion Hospers

Mr. Hospers was associated with the Sioux Abstract Company for many years and was also active in the farm loan and life insurance business. Mrs. Hospers was active in the musical life of the community, including directing the Farm Bureau Chorus and being director of the American Reformed Church Choir.

Sunday School Class American Reformed Church–1910. Teacher, County Supt. of Schools, Mr. F. E. Fuller
Front row, left to right: Carl Hospers; Fred Slob; Kate Klay Smith; Esther Maris Draayom; Jake Wobbema; Ray Casjens.
Second row: David Bogaard; Kate Balkema Wilson; Gertrude Van Pelt Stadt; Anne Snyder; Freeman Lohr.
Third row: Chas. Vander Sluis; Magdalene Synhorst; Effie Dykstra Klay; Lydia Schalekamp Noteboom; Amy Schalekamp McNutt; Hubert De Booy.
Fourth row: Mr. F. E. Fuller; Matt De Booy; Milton Staft; Arthur Vande Steeg; Peter Wobbema.

Mr. and Mrs. Hendrik De Jong

HENDRIK DE JONG
Orange City Area Pioneer

In 1847 Hendrik De Jong, son of Mr. and Mrs. Koenraad De Jong, emigrated with his parents From Holland to Marion County, Iowa.

He left Marion County in 1871 to settle in Northwest Iowa where he homesteaded southwest of Orange City. The original farm has been operated continuously by members of the family through four generations to date.

Koenraad H. De Jong took over in 1898. He specialized in raisng Clydesdale draft horses with seed stock imported from Scotland. He also founded a herd of Polled Hereford (hornless) cattle.

In 1921 his son Julius took over, and at the present time his grandson Koenraad is operating the farm.

Keyron Schumacher
Pressman

**CENTENNIAL
BOOK
PRODUCTION
STAFF**

Fred Brandes
Composition

Rev. E. Van Engelenhoven
Editor

Harvey Pluim
Publisher

Edward Stetson
Design

STAFF

The following are names of people that helped produce the Cenntennial Book:

Writing the history of Orange City:
    Mrs. Simon Vande Garde

Writing the "Tulip Time" story:
    Arie Vander Stoep

Gathering pictures:
    Mrs. Martin Vander Maaten Sr.
    Miss Geraldine Reinders
    Mrs. Franklin De Haan

Typing:
    Mrs. Elmer Hofmeyer
    Mrs. Merlyn Vander Broek

Editing:
    Attorney John D. Te Paske
    Dr. Howard Schutter
    Mr. William Top

Photography:
    Mr. Edward Stetson
    Mr. Keyron Schumacher

Co-ordinators:
    Rev. E. Van Engelenhoven
    Mr. Allen Faber

This book is an incomplete recording of the history of the first century of Orange City. It does, however, give a glimpse of the courage, industry, integrity, hopes, prayers and spiritual depth of the pioneers who claimed the spot that Orange City occupies.

With Samuel of old we exclaim, "EBENEZER"; "Hitherto hath the Lord helped us."

(I Samuel 7:12)

Published by
The Ad-Visor
Orange City, Iowa
2.5 M – May 1970